THE EVERYTHING

PARENT'S GUIDE TO

EATING DISORDERS

Dear Reader,

Eating disorders have affected my life in more ways than I ever would have imagined. There was a time when the only thing I knew about eating disorders was what I had read. That was before. Before eating disorders affected people I love and almost took my life.

Recovery is possible. The journey through an eating disorder may well be the most difficult struggle one can encounter. The only path more difficult may be if one's own child is facing an eating disorder. It hurts to watch one's child literally unable to face eating. The emotional roller coaster is difficult to describe and ranges from fear and frustration to heartache and even anger.

My message to both you and your child you love is twofold. First, don't give up; never stop fighting. Second, the best you can do is enough, and there is no room for blame on this battlefield. Love, love, love.

Wishing you joy, comfort, and peace,

Angie Best-Boss

WELCOME TO THE
EVERYTHING®
PARENT'S GUIDES

Everything® Parent's Guides are a part of the bestselling Everything® series and cover common parenting issues like childhood illnesses and tantrums, as well as medical conditions like asthma and juvenile diabetes. These family-friendly books are designed to be a one-stop guide for parents. If you want authoritative information on specific topics not fully covered in other books, Everything® Parent's Guides are your perfect solution.

 Alerts

Urgent warnings

 Facts

Important snippets of information

 Essentials

Quick handy tips

 Questions

Answers to common questions

When you're done reading, you can finally say you know **EVERYTHING®**!

PUBLISHER Karen Cooper

DIRECTOR OF ACQUISITIONS AND INNOVATION Paula Munier

MANAGING EDITOR, EVERYTHING® SERIES Lisa Laing

COPY CHIEF Casey Ebert

ASSISTANT PRODUCTION EDITOR Melanie Cordova

ACQUISITIONS EDITOR Brett Palana-Shanahan

SENIOR DEVELOPMENT EDITOR Brett Palana-Shanahan

EDITORIAL ASSISTANT Ross Weisman

EVERYTHING® SERIES COVER DESIGNER Erin Alexander

LAYOUT DESIGNERS Erin Dawson, Michelle Roy Kelly, Elisabeth Lariviere, Denise Wallace

Visit the entire Everything® series at *www.everything.com*

THE

EVERYTHING

PARENT'S GUIDE TO

EATING
DISORDERS

The information you need to see
the warning signs, help promote
positive body image, and develop
a recovery plan for your child

Angie Best-Boss, MA
Content Editor, EatingDisordersOnline.com

adamsmedia
Avon, Massachusetts

An Everything® Series Book.
Everything® and everything.com® are registered trademarks of F+W Media, Inc.

Published by Adams Media, a division of F+W Media, Inc.
57 Littlefield Street, Avon, MA 02322 U.S.A.
www.adamsmedia.com

ISBN 10: 1-4405-2785-7
ISBN 13: 978-1-4405- 2785-2
eISBN 10: 1-4405-2886-1
eISBN 13: 978-1-4405-2886-6

Printed in the United States of America.

10 9 8 7 6 5 4 3 2 1

Library of Congress Cataloging-in-Publication Data
is available from the publisher.

This publication is designed to provide accurate and authoritative information with regard to the subject matter covered. It is sold with the understanding that the publisher is not engaged in rendering legal, accounting, or other professional advice. If legal advice or other expert assistance is required, the services of a competent professional person should be sought.
—From a *Declaration of Principles* jointly adopted by a Committee of the American Bar Association and a Committee of Publishers and Associations

This book is intended as general information only, and should not be used to diagnose or treat any health condition. In light of the complex, individual, and specific nature of health problems, this book is not intended to replace professional medical advice. The ideas, procedures, and suggestions in this book are intended to supplement, not replace, the advice of a trained medical professional. Consult your physician before adopting any of the suggestions in this book, as well as about any condition that may require diagnosis or medical attention. The author and publisher disclaim any liability arising directly or indirectly from the use of this book.

Many of the designations used by manufacturers and sellers to distinguish their products are claimed as trademarks. Where those designations appear in this book and Adams Media was aware of a trademark claim, the designations have been printed with initial capital letters.

This book is available at quantity discounts for bulk purchases.
For information, please call 1-800-289-0963.

Dedication

Dedicated to Terry and Kim Moore of Nonviolent Alternatives (www.nonviolentalternatives.com), for saving my life and helping me heal.

Acknowledgments

I am grateful for the dozens of professionals, parents, and children who shared their insight, expertise, and personal stories. A few of the professionals I am indebted to include Ashley Solomon, PsyD (*www.nourishing-the-soul.com*); Margarita Tartakovsky, MS (*http://blogs.psychcentral.com/weightless*); Rosie Molinary (*www.rosiemolinary.com*), author of *Beautiful You: A Daily Guide to Radical Self-Acceptance* and *Hijas Americanas: Beauty, Body Image, and Growing Up Latina*; Diane Keddy, MS, RD, FAED (*www.dianekeddy.com*); Katja Rowell, MD (*www.familyfeedingdynamics.com*); and Laura Stern (*www.laurenlazarstern.com*), author of *The Slender Trap: A Food and Body Workbook*.

eat·ing dis·or·der

(eˈtĭng dĭs-ôrˈdər) ▶

n. **1.** Serious, potentially life-threatening, biologically based mental illness, usually characterized by daily functioning affected by disordered body image, a preoccupation with and anxiety related to food and eating, and disordered eating.

Contents

Introduction

Eating disorders are a prevalent and dangerous disease that affects millions of children, adolescents, and adults and can begin as young as six years old. Eating disorders can affect anyone, regardless of gender, race, age, or economic level or religious belief system. They have been found in every country in the world. It is a growing problem across all age groups.

Eating disorders are not easy to define, either. From starving oneself through anorexia nervosa, binge eating, binging and purging in bulimia, to night eating or having diabetes and refusing insulin in order to lose weight, the sheer range of potential disordered eating behaviors can feel overwhelming. What is a parent supposed to do?

First, parents must understand that while an eating disorder requires mental health treatment, it is a medical problem that often requires medical treatment. The longer an eating disorder continues, the greater the likelihood that significant medical problems will develop and may even be fatal. To make an accurate diagnosis and treatment even more challenging, many eating disorder sufferers have coexisting conditions, including depression, anxiety, self-mutilation, or substance abuse.

There is no such thing as a harmless eating disorder. A child does not have to be emaciated or even underweight for health problems to occur. After all, an overweight child who has a binge eating disorder has significant emotional and physical issues that need attention.

Eating disorders are biologically based mental illness and fully treatable with a combination of nutritional, medical, and therapeutic supports. However, getting a diagnosis and finding appropriate, evidence-based treatment is often a challenge.

Parents do not cause eating disorders, and if a health care provider or mental health specialist indicates otherwise, run to the nearest exit and seek treatment providers who are better informed regarding eating disorder research and treatment. Parents do, however, play a powerful role in their children's recovery. And recovery is possible, even with a child or adolescent who insists there is not a problem and does not want to get help.

Some parents discover their child's eating disorder fairly early and are able to begin treatment quickly without needing medical intervention, while others may not be aware of their child's disorder until it has become an entrenched problem with medical problems that must be addressed before the eating disorder can be treated. Parental involvement is crucial at every stage of the eating disorder treatment process, regardless of how far the disease has progressed.

When a parent first becomes aware of his or her child's eating disorder, that moment is the time to act. It will likely take a great deal of time, energy, research, frustration, and, in some cases, financial resources to adequately treat the child. However, the research is clear—when parents are actively involved in treatment, children with eating disorders are more likely to recover and avoid relapse.

Children with an eating disorder need their parents to be prepared, engaged, knowledgeable, and ready to do battle on their behalf.

CHAPTER 1

Know the Enemy: Understanding Eating Disorders

E ating disorders are serious, life-threatening brain disorders that can cause long-term health effects. Eating disorders are difficult to understand and sometimes easy to miss, and due to our culture's misconceptions, you may fail to recognize the danger signs in your own child. There are many different ways that eating disorders can manifest, and parents need to understand the different types of eating disorders and the dangers they pose. As with any disease, early identification greatly improves treatment outcomes.

What Are Eating Disorders?

An eating disorder can mean any type of disordered eating, from not eating to binging and purging to a dozen variations on the theme. The American Psychiatric Association's indicators for an eating disorder include a preoccupation with food, anxiety related to food and eating, disordered eating, and a body image distortion, all of which can affect a person's functioning in daily life. Eating disorders are brain disorders and are usually characterized by children adamantly denying that anything is wrong, even when they are clearly suffering from malnutrition, are eating overly excessive amounts of food in one sitting, or are refusing to eat at all.

The Origins

Typically, eating disorders start when children are young, sometimes as young as four but often not until adolescence. However, an eating disorder can begin at any age, even into middle age or later in life. Eating disorders are not, as commonly thought, an attempt of a child to gain control over his or her life or to exert control over the parents, nor are they the outcome of an overly controlling parent. Eating disorders are a brain disorder that may manifest at any point in a person's life. Brain chemistry, function, and structure in patients with eating disorders are different from the brains of those without an eating disorder.

Who Is Affected?

Statistics from the U.S. Department of Health and Human Services indicate that teenagers are not the only ones who develop eating disorders. In fact, the number of children under the age of twelve who are admitted to the hospital for eating disorders skyrocketed over 119 percent from 1996 to 2006. Eating disorders now account for 4 percent of all hospitalizations in children. There are some personality traits such as perfectionism or inflexibility that may indicate a predisposition to developing an eating disorder.

Anorexia Nervosa

Anorexia nervosa is an eating disorder characterized by an excessive desire to limit food intake. Usually accompanied by body image disturbance, most sufferers have a misperception of their body size and shape. Anorexia nervosa typically begins by age thirteen and is preceded by dieting behavior. Many people with anorexia have a strong need to be around food, either by cooking or serving it.

Anorexia Symptoms

A young person who has anorexia often displays a number of typical signs and symptoms, including:

- Dramatic weight loss with no known medical reason or illness
- Preoccupation with food, weight, size, calories, fat grams, and dieting
- Refusal to eat certain foods, which may progress to restrictions against entire food categories, such as carbohydrates
- Frequent comments about feeling fat or overweight despite weight loss or body weight
- Denial of hunger, even when no food has been eaten
- Developing food rituals such as excessive chewing, eating foods in certain orders, or rearranging food on a plate
- Consistent avoidance of situations that involve food, especially mealtimes
- Excessive and rigid exercise regimens regardless of weather, illness, fatigue, or injury; strong need to burn off calories taken in
- Social isolation and withdrawal from usual friends and activities
- Behaviors and attitudes indicating that weight loss, dieting, and control of food are becoming primary concerns
- Deterioration of academic performance
- Pronounced emotional changes including irritability, hostility, suspiciousness, intolerance, and secretiveness
- Wearing oversized clothing to hide thinness

Health Consequences of Anorexia

Anorexia nervosa is a form of self-starvation. Because the body is denied most of the essential vitamins and nutrients it needs to function normally, an anorexic's body must then slow down its processes in a desperate attempt to conserve energy. When the body's systems slow down, there can be a number of serious medical consequences. About half of the people who have had anorexia will develop bulimia or bulimic patterns.

 **Question**

What's a normal calorie intake for children?
In children ages six to twelve, 1,800–2,200 calories are needed, while in adolescents, 1,900–2,500 calories a day are needed for adequate nutrition and growth. A variety of foods, including proteins, fat, carbohydrates, fruits, and vegetables, should be eaten regularly.

According to the National Institute of Mental Health, physical consequences that might be seen in a child with anorexia include:

- Because the heart muscle is changing, very low blood pressure and an abnormally slow heart rate often result
- Dry, brittle bones
- Muscle weakness and loss
- Severe dehydration that may lead to kidney failure
- Overall weakness, fainting, and fatigue
- Hair loss; dry hair and skin
- In an effort to preserve body heat, there is sometimes a growth of lanugo, a downy layer of hair all over the body and face
- Dry and yellowish skin
- Severe constipation
- Drop in internal body temperature, causing a person to feel cold all the time
- Lethargy

 Fact

Anorexia is the third most common chronic illness among adolescents, and the mortality rate associated with anorexia nervosa is twelve times higher than the death rate associated with all causes of death for females fifteen to twenty-four years old.

Bulimia Nervosa

Bulimia is an eating disorder characterized by episodes of binge eating followed by some form of purging or restriction. Binges can be defined as secretive periods of unusually rapid consumption of high-caloric foods. Typically, bulimics will follow binging with self-induced vomiting. Sometimes, however, the purging, or ridding the body of the food, will involve laxative use, an emetic agent (one that induces vomiting), or using a diuretic (which increases the volume of urine excreted), fasting, or excessive exercise.

While it may seem difficult to understand, purging behavior serves to relieve anxiety and reduce stress. However, this binge and purge cycle is usually accompanied by depression, an awareness that the eating disorder is abnormal and out of control, which leads to self-deprecating thoughts. The illness often goes undetected by others for years because most bulimics are within a normal weight range.

"My entire life revolves around bulimia. It is my high. It is my addiction. It makes me feel like I am on top of the world. It is who I am. The best way to describe my bulimia is that it fills a hole in my soul. I am scared. I know that I need to stop, but I just don't care anymore. Somewhere along the way I lost myself in the midst of all this eating and throwing up. I am scared of who I am without it. I am bulimic," says Dani, who began purging at twelve years old.

 Essential

Children are not free from risk once they leave home. In fact, one-fourth of all college-aged women engage in binging and purging as a weight-management technique. Some college students have binge/purge parties where they eat a large quantity of "bad" or high-calorie food, then they each vomit. They might also share diet pills, laxatives, and diuretics, increasing the risks of young adults who may already be vulnerable to developing an eating disorder.

Most bulimia sufferers are female, but men may develop bulimia as well. It affects 1–3 percent of middle- and high-school girls and 1–4 percent of college-age women, and it usually develops in early to middle adolescence. Like anorexia, bulimia is usually preceded by dieting behavior, and self-evaluation is unduly influenced by size and weight, although body misperception is not typically present.

Bulimia Symptoms

If your child has bulimia, you may notice excessive amounts of food missing, missing money (used to purchase food), hidden food wrappers or receipts, as well as frequent bathroom trips following meals. A person with bulimia often vomits within the first thirty minutes of eating but may be able to vomit up to two hours later. A bulimic may use her finger, a utensil, or toothbrush to induce vomiting, or, after time, a bulimic can train him or herself to vomit at will.

 Alert

Some bulimics will use syrup of ipecac as a means to induce vomiting. Once a staple in many families' first-aid kits in case of accidental poisoning, few drugstores now carry it. However, it can easily be purchased online without a prescription and used by bulimics.

According to the World Health Organization, the criteria for a diagnosis of bulimia nervosa include the following:

- Persistent preoccupation with eating and an irresistible craving for food
- Episodes of overeating in which large amounts of food are consumed in short periods of time
- Excessive exercise
- Induced vomiting after eating

- Starving for periods of time
- Taking medicines such as laxatives to counteract the binging
- Fear of obesity

Long-Term Health Consequences

A bulimic will almost always have severe tooth decay and damage as a result of the frequency of stomach acids that are released during frequent vomiting. For those who abuse laxatives, chronic irregular bowel movements and constipation are common. Bulimia has the potential to cause severe physical damage to a person's health, especially with regards to electrolyte imbalances, which are caused by dehydration and potassium and sodium loss from the body as a result of purging behaviors. Those electrolyte imbalances can lead to irregular heartbeats and heart failure and death.

Other potential consequences include the potential for the rupture of the esophagus from frequent vomiting, and the stomach can even rupture during periods of binging. Peptic ulcers and pancreatitis are also common.

Binge Eating Disorder

It isn't clear how many young people have binge eating disorder (BED), as its prevalence in the general population is still unclear. Researchers estimate that approximately one-fourth of all obese individuals have frequent episodes of binge eating, though people who struggle with binge eating disorder can be of normal weight. As with other eating disorders, it affects women more frequently than men.

Many people who suffer from binge eating disorder have a history of depression, and, as with other eating disorders, people who struggle with binge eating disorder very often express shame, guilt, and distress over their eating behaviors.

Binge Eating Disorder Symptoms

Binge eating is the most common eating disorder, though parents tend to know the least about it. While the American Psychiatric Association's (APA) *Diagnostic and Statistical Manual of Mental Disorders* (DSM-IV) does not yet have a specific category for binge eating disorder, it does list diagnostic criteria. According to the DSM-IV, binge eating disorder is characterized by several behavioral and emotional signs, including:

- Recurrent episodes of binge eating occurring at least twice a week for six months
- Eating a larger amount of food than normal during a short time frame (any two-hour period)
- Lack of control over eating during the binge episode (such as feeling you can't stop eating or control what or how much you are eating)

There are other signs of binge eating disorder (BED) that are not listed in the DSM but may be seen in people with BED, including:

- Eating alone
- Feelings of guilt, disgust, or shame after a binge
- Purging is not done, though the binging behaviors are similar

When a person with bulimia or binge eating disorder binges, the amount of food that the person ingests can be surprisingly large. In fact, some fatalities have occurred when a binge eater's stomach has ruptured. It is not uncommon for a family member to get upset when a significant amount of food is eaten. Some families must use a locked cabinet to keep food protected from a child with an eating disorder.

Here is an example of one young person's afternoon binge:

- Breakfast bar
- Yogurt smoothie
- Chicken pita with cheese and fries
- Slice of pecan pie
- Three donuts
- Twelve donut holes
- Two chicken wings
- A hot dog with bun
- Salad
- A large slice of three-layer German chocolate cake
- Two-liter bottle of soda

Your child's binges may be much smaller than this and still count as a binge if it is a larger than normal amount of food.

Long-Term Health Consequences

A person with binge eating disorder is at risk for a number of long-term health consequences, though these dangers are more likely to affect harm over years or even decades when compared to anorexia and bulimia. Binge eating disorder often results in a number of the health risks associated with clinical obesity, including:

- High blood pressure
- High cholesterol levels
- Heart disease as a result of elevated triglyceride levels
- Type 2 diabetes
- Gallbladder disease

Short-Term Consequences

One of the differences between binge eating disorder and bulimia and anorexia is that it is more obvious when a person is suffering from binge eating disorder, often because the person is overweight or even obese. For children and teenagers, a hostile school environment can exacerbate the young person's issues, and she may then binge more to compensate for the bad feelings.

Body Dysmorphic Disorder

Body dysmorphic disorder (BDD) is characterized by extreme, persistently negative views about one's body, and it is sometimes known as "imagined ugliness." It is included because research has not yet decided whether BDD is an eating disorder in its own right or if it always accompanies an eating disorder. BDD may seem like a minor issue, but it is a serious illness that occurs when a person is preoccupied with minor or imaginary physical flaws, usually of the skin, hair, and nose. Typically, BDD involves focuses not on minor flaws but on perceived flaws. Body dysmorphic disorder is also known as dysmorphophobia—the fear of having a deformity.

Signs and Symptoms of Body Dysmorphic Disorder

What teenager doesn't look in the mirror a lot? BDD is not the same thing. When a child has this disorder, he or she will spend hours staring in the mirror, looking for every flaw. The staring often leads to crying, even screaming. Eventually, people who have this disorder are more likely to have, or at least want to have, multiple cosmetic surgery procedures, often spending thousands of dollars on unnecessary procedures. The surgeries, of course, do not "solve" the problem. Other signs include:

- Belief that others take special notice of your appearance in a negative way
- The need to seek reassurance about your appearance from others
- Excessive grooming, such as hair plucking
- Extreme self-consciousness
- Refusal to appear in pictures

- Skin picking
- Comparison of your appearance with that of others
- Wearing excessive makeup or clothing to camouflage perceived flaws

Bigorexia

Bigorexia, officially known as muscle dysmorphia, is considered to be a variant (or subtype) of body dysmorphic disorder. It is an obsession with being muscular and is seen primarily in men, although it can occur in women as well. It may manifest itself through excessive working out, taking supplements, and consistent worrying about not being big enough, even if the person has well-developed muscles. Other names for the disorder include reverse anorexia and the Adonis complex.

Signs and symptoms of bigorexia include:

- Distorted self-image
- Missing social events, skipping work, and cancelling plans with family/friends to work out
- Never being satisfied with the muscular mass of one's body
- Maintaining a strict high-protein and low-fat diet
- Using excessive amounts of food supplements
- Frequently looking at one's self in the mirror
- Steroid abuse, unnecessary plastic surgery, and even suicide
- Avoiding situations where one's body might be exposed
- Working out despite an injury
- Maintaining extreme workout methods

Eating Disorders Not Otherwise Specified

Eating disorders not otherwise specified, sometimes referred to as EDNOS, are eating disorders that require treatment but do not cleanly and neatly fit into a specific eating disorder. It does not, however, mean that such disorders do not require treatment or are less serious. According to the DSM-IV, EDNOS has these characteristics:

- The individual still has regular menses (periods), though all other qualifications for anorexia nervosa are met.
- A normal weight is still maintained, despite continuous weight loss due to food restriction.
- All other requirements for bulimia nervosa are met except binging occurs only once a week for three months or less.
- Inappropriate compensatory behavior, such as purging, occurs after eating small amounts of food. A normal body weight is still maintained.
- Large amounts of food are frequently chewed and spit out, without swallowing.
- Binge eating occurs without the use of inappropriate compensatory behaviors such as purging.

Other types of eating disorders, such as diabulimia and orthorexia nervosa, are not yet currently recognized as mental disorders in any of the medical manuals such as the *International Classification of Diseases* (ICD-10) or the DSM-IV.

Chew and Spit
The practice of chewing and spitting is one in which a person tastes the food, chews it, and then spits it out. It can be a part of anorexia, and it can also be a part of a person's entry into disordered eating. Part of the problem is that seeing, smelling, and tasting food creates an excess of insulin. Insulin increases appetite, which makes the person feel hungry and creates a vicious cycle.

Diabulimia
About 40 percent of fifteen- to thirty-year-old diabetics regularly manipulate or omit insulin in order to lose weight. Though it isn't an official eating disorder, the practice has been named *diab-*

ulimia. Eating disorders among insulin-dependent diabetics is estimated to be two to six times higher than in the general population, with up to 25 percent of females having a diagnosable eating disorder. Type 1 diabetes and eating disorders are, individually, very serious diseases. When combined, they can be even more dangerous and lead to staph infections, dehydration, neuropathy, a stroke, or even death.

 Essential

For support and information on this disorder, contact DWED (Diabetics with Eating Disorders), a nonprofit organization, at *www.dwed.org.uk* or check out the Diabulimia Helpline at *www.diabulimiahelpline.org* or call: (425) 985-3635.

Symptoms of diabulimia, also referred to as ED-DMT, include:

- High HbA1c (glycated hemoglobin)
- Reluctance or refusal to do blood sugar tests
- Severe fluctuations in weight
- Frequent urinary tract infections or thrush
- Requests to frequently change meal plans
- Distress or fear of injecting
- Refusal to inject or requires privacy to inject
- Diabetes complications
- Co-occurrence of depression, anxiety, or borderline personality disorder

Orthorexia Nervosa

Orthorexia comes from the Greek word *orthos*, meaning "correct or right," with *orexis*, meaning "appetite." Orthorexia refers to people who are so obsessive about eating healthfully that they risk their lives through extreme diets and fitness routines. An example could be when a person chooses to stop eating red meat but then eventually decides to cut out all meat. Then he might eliminate all processed foods, and then will eat only specific foods that are prepared in very specific ways. While this may seem harmless, the restrictions can be overwhelming and narrowed down to only a few raw foods. For example, root vegetables may get eliminated because they contain carbohydrates, and even apples may be deemed toxic if they aren't from an approved organic grower.

 Alert

In an effort to educate parents and other caregivers about the full scope of eating disorders, there may be information in this book that a child might use to further her eating disorder, particularly related to how children often hide problematic behaviors and thinking. Children and young adults struggling with an eating disorder could use portions of this book to further entrench themselves in the disease. This is not a book to leave lying around.

Orthorexia can easily develop into another eating disorder. Experts say the disorder affects one in ten women—usually in their thirties—and one in twenty men. It can, however, affect teenagers, and athletes are particularly likely to fall prey.

Night Eating

Night eating is otherwise known as sleep-related eating (disorder), nocturnal sleep-related eating disorder (NS-RED), and sleep-eating syndrome. Sleepwalking is often involved in people with a sleep-eating disorder, while people with night eating disorder literally cannot sleep unless they engage in excessive nocturnal overeating, also called compulsive hyperphagia. Night eating or drinking is diagnosed when 50 percent or more of an individual's diet is consumed between sleeping hours, and eating may occur once or many times during the night. Children and teens with night eating are likely to be overweight.

Signs and symptoms of night eating include:

- Little or no appetite for breakfast
- Eating more after dinner than for dinner, with more than half of the daily food intake being consumed after dinner. Eating is not binging but continuous throughout the evening hours.
- Pattern persisting at least two months
- Difficulty sleeping
- Eating produces feelings of guilt, anxiety, or shame

Selective Eating/Restricting

Some people become obsessed about certain types of food, parts of food, or even the timing of when food is eaten. For example, Paul, a fifteen-year-old, is terrified of eating after 5 P.M. If anything (food or drink) touches his lips, he is convinced that he will choke to death. "It's as though someone or something takes over my body. No matter what you say to me or how you try to explain how ridiculous or crazy that sounds, I can't help it. I know it's crazy, but in the same way, I also know it to be absolutely true."

Another eating disorder that is making the rounds on college campuses and some high-school campuses but has not yet made it into a diagnostic manual is drinkorexia. With drinkorexia, students and young adults eat significantly less than their bodies need in order to conserve calories so they can drink more alcohol. Alcoholism and eating disorders frequently occur together and often co-occur in the presence of other personality and psychiatric disorders according to the National Institute of Alcohol Abuse and Alcoholism. Research published in the *Journal of Alcohol and Drug Education* studied more than 600 freshmen at one university and found that 14 percent of students restrict calories before they drink alcohol. Of those students, 70 percent were women.

Coexisting Disorders

Individuals with an eating disorder often have other conditions at the same time. When that happens, they are referred to as *co-occurring, coexisting,* or *comorbid* conditions. It is important that coexisting conditions are considered in the evaluation and treatment of eating disorders. The most common disorders to occur with eating disorders are self-mutilation, depression, anxiety, and bipolar disorder. More than half the affected teens had depression, anxiety, or some other mental disorder. A significant number of teens with eating disorders also reported suicidal thoughts or suicide attempts.

Personality Disorders

A personality disorder often develops in adolescence or early adulthood, and it involves consistent patterns of perceiving and relating to others, as well as thinking about oneself, that are inflexible and maladaptive. Over 40 percent of anorexia nervosa/bulimia nervosa patients have comorbid personality disorders, usually narcissistic, histrionic, antisocial, and borderline personality disorders. Bulimics are more likely to have borderline personality disorder.

Depression and Anxiety

Mood disorders, such as major depression or bipolar disorder, and anxiety disorders can often accompany eating disorders. Reports indicate that 59 percent of those with bulimia and 80 percent of those with the purging type of bulimia have accompanying depression. Any children or teens diagnosed with an eating disorder should also have a thorough psychological evaluation.

Symptoms of depression include:

- Declining performance at school
- Lack of interest in friends or activities previously enjoyed
- An overall sadness or expressions of hopelessness

- Restlessness, agitation, anger, or rage
- Decreased energy level
- Lack of self-esteem
- Decreased concentration or memory
- Changes in eating or sleeping
- Abusing substances
- Suicidal thoughts or gestures

 Fact

Many people with eating disorders have partial symptom syndrome, where most of the DSM-IV diagnostic criteria are met but the condition may or may not develop into full-blown anorexia, bulimia, or another eating disorder.

Obsessive-Compulsive Disorder

Obsessive-compulsive disorder, or OCD, is a neurobiological anxiety disorder characterized by compulsions and obsessions that typically take up an excessive amount of time, usually up to an hour or more each day, and create a significant amount of distress. Rigid thinking, inflexibility, and an insistence on perfectionism are all common manifestations as well. About a third of OCD cases will begin in childhood, and there is a strong link with eating disorders. About 10–13 percent of people who have obsessive-compulsive disorder will also have an eating disorder.

CHAPTER 2

Myths and Misconceptions about Eating Disorders

E ating disorders don't discriminate. Anyone can suffer from an ED, regardless of age, race, socioeconomic status, or gender. No one is immune. When parents, coaches, and teachers believe outdated perceptions, then it becomes too easy for children and teens with active eating disorders to slip through the cracks. The longer that eating disorders persist, the more difficult they are to treat and the greater the risk for long-term physical problems, even death.

It Only Affects Rich, White Girls

One of the most damaging misconceptions about eating disorders is that they only occur among upper-middle-class white teenagers. While there are plenty of young ladies in the socioeconomic group who do suffer from disordered eating, they don't corner the market. Children of both genders, of all ages, of all ethnic and cultural groups, and from all socioeconomic backgrounds are vulnerable to eating disorders. The danger of believing that eating disorders only affect certain segments of the population means that too often parents, teachers, coaches, and others may miss the signs and symptoms of an eating disorder because a child doesn't fit into the typical mold.

In fact, one parent explained, "I had never heard of a boy having an eating disorder. The first time my wife suggested it was a possibility, I laughed at her. I honestly didn't think it was even possible. I think if we had known how common it truly is, we might have been better able to see the signs before our son's health was at risk. No one else saw it, either. Not our family doctor, not his coach . . . we never considered the possibility of an eating disorder until (our son) was really sick."

Manorexia

Eating disorders aren't just for girls anymore. Women are much more likely than men to develop an eating disorder. That doesn't mean, however, that boys and men are immune. In fact, a Harvard study found that one-quarter of those with eating disorders and 40 percent of binge eaters were male. Men who participate in athletics that require weigh-ins, such as wrestling, boxing, and crew, are most susceptible to extreme exercise and eating regimens.

 Fact

Common Sense Media offers these startling statistics: Nearly a third of teen boys try to control their weight through unhealthy methods, like taking laxatives or smoking. One in eight boys ages twelve to eighteen reported using hormones or supplements to change their appearance, improve muscle mass, or gain more strength.

Jeremy Gillitzer, a model who was interviewed shortly before his death from bulimia, wrote on his blog, "*Guess Who? My hair is falling out and growing on my body . . . to keep me warm. My gums are receding. My reproductive system is dormant . . . or dead. I am hunchbacked because my muscles cannot support my neck. I am extremely constipated. I have a bedsore on my tailbone from the friction. An 80-year-old lady, you ask? No, a 35-year-old man.*"

Eating Disorders Differ by Gender

Patrick Bergstrom, an advocate for men with eating disorders, describes the common symptoms that men with an eating disorder may have:

- Perfectionist attitude
- Overexercising
- Substance abuse
- Strong fixation on appearance and athletic performance
- Isolation
- Mood swings
- People pleaser
- All-or-nothing mind-set
- Loss of interest in friends and family
- Denial
- Overuse of supplements or performance-enhancing drugs

Treatment and Gender

There are a number of factors that makes diagnosis and treatment for men difficult. Health care providers are less likely to identify eating disorders in men, and many of the diagnostic tools for eating disorders are designed for women. Men are less likely to seek treatment because having an eating disorder is perceived as being feminine, but even when they do, there are few treatment programs designed specifically for men.

Adolescents Only Need Apply

Eating disorders most commonly affect teenagers, though it can be difficult to identify exactly when an eating disorder begins because others may not become aware of it for months, or sometimes years, if the young person is particularly adept at hiding symptoms. Eating disorders can begin at any age, even among the elderly. It is important to recognize that middle-aged adults can have eating disorders that are lingering from years prior or have a new onset.

 Fact

This is a marathon, not a sprint. Consider your child's eating disorder a chronic disease that will require treatment for an extended period of time. Approximately 75–80 percent suffer with these disorders for one to fifteen years.

Children

This will be covered in greater detail in Chapter 3, but children as young as four have been identified as having a diagnosable eating disorder. Children younger than four may have eating issues, but those are typically related primarily to other physical or psychological problems. A child or young adult may well be influenced by having a parent, teacher, coach, or other important adult who has an eating disorder. If a parent has an eating disorder, it may increase the likelihood that a child will develop an eating disorder.

Whites Only

People of color are not a group who are able to dodge the body dissatisfaction bullet or eating disorders. "Every day, those of us not rooted in the dominant culture in some way navigate a society that was not created with us in mind. We confront our different cultures, our varying traditions, the different values before us— and we try to carve out a place for ourselves. Given that so many people are on the margins once you really look at what the standard for beauty is in this country, how many people can really be completely immune from the possibility of body dissatisfaction," explains Rosie Molinary, author of *Hijas Americanas: Beauty, Body Image, and Growing Up Latina*.

Minorities

The truth is that disordered eating habits—of all types—are not the province of only the white culture. African-American young women are just as likely to engage in eating disorders, especially bulimia and anorexia nervosa. Other research indicates:

- Rates of minorities with eating disorders are similar to those of white women.
- 74 percent of Native-American girls reported dieting and purging with diet pills.
- 53.5 percent of African-American females were at risk of an eating disorder (according to respondents in a reader survey in *Essence* magazine).
- For young women in Japan, eating disorders are one of the most common psychological problems they face.

Eating disorders among different ethnic groups may present differently and make it more likely that health care providers will miss early signs and symptoms. For example, Margarita Alegria, PhD, director of the Center for Multicultural Mental Health Research at Cambridge Health Alliance, suggests that women of color may bring up weight control to their health care providers but not concerns about their body dissatisfaction or image. That distinction may be enough for health care providers who are not culturally sensitive to miss early cues.

 Fact

While African-American women are less likely than white women to have anorexia nervosa, more African-American women report using laxatives, diuretics, and fasting to control weight gain.

Religion as Protection

Among some people who have a strong spiritual belief, there is sometimes the perception that having faith or raising their child within a spiritual community may protect their child from outside influences, including those surrounding body image and self-esteem. But because eating disorders are not simply a result of seeing too many thin models and are instead a brain disorder, spiritual practices alone cannot protect against an eating disorder any more than one's faith can protect one's child from cancer. While belonging to a faith community may provide numerous benefits and support, there is no evidence that belonging to a spiritual group can prevent your child from developing an eating disorder. Children representing all faith groups have developed eating disorders. However, for many, a spiritual community may be beneficial in recovery.

Religious Practices

The link between food and faith has long been reported, even as far back as the Middle Ages where girls and women practiced *anorexia mirabilis*, or starving themselves "in the name of God." While it is hardly common practice today, abstaining from or gorging on food is a part of many faith traditions, from potluck suppers to fasting. While a child with a predisposition to an eating disorder may be better able to self-starve during a period of fasting, there is no evidence that suggests any spiritual practice is the cause.

 Fact

No single faith group is exempt from eating disorders. In one study, one in nineteen Orthodox Jewish teenage girls in Brooklyn had an eating disorder—about 50 percent higher than the general population. The Philadelphia-based Renfrew Center is one of the few centers in the United States that offers treatment specifically for Orthodox Jewish sufferers.

But They Don't Look Thin

There's the misconception that someone with an eating disorder always looks frail and loses a lot of weight. But this isn't always the case. Someone with bulimia, for instance, may not show the signs of weight loss. She or he may even look healthy. Someone's appearance doesn't reveal how much that person is suffering or the damage it's doing to his or her body. On average, about 70 percent of women who have an eating disorder are at what is considered to be a healthy weight. A lower or higher weight than average is not proof that a person has an eating disorder.

 Alert

Your child is not safe just because he or she is not emaciated. Be on the lookout for signs of an eating disorder in your child that may not be weight related at all. Signs of bulimia, for example, may include swollen cheeks, overly clear teeth, bad breath, and broken blood vessels in the eyes.

A person who could be described as very thin may have a very healthy relationship with food, while a person who seems to be a "normal" size may be in the midst of battling an agonizing eating disorder. Everyone, at any size, requires and deserves treatment if they're suffering from an eating disorder.

Obesity

Not all children and teens who are overweight have an eating disorder, but being overweight and/or dieting may precede an eating disorder, especially binge eating disorder or bulimia. Obesity sometimes accompanies bulimia and night eating disorder but is often found in binge eating disorder. If your child is overweight, it is important to monitor your child for signs of an eating disorder or changes in mood or personality.

It's about Control

Even though it may feel differently to the patient and to the patient's family, eating disorders are not a disease of choice, nor are they a way to attempt to control others. One misunderstanding many people have, and this isn't just parents, is that people just can't grasp why someone with anorexia, for example, can't eat. They wonder what the big deal is and often see not eating as a willful action. But eating disorders are much more complicated than that.

Understanding Choices

Carolyn Costin, founder and director of Monte Nido Treatment Center, says that what makes the idea of choice versus illness in eating disorders is that we see people choose to go on a diet. We see people choose to exercise. We see the choices people make and then we ultimately end up thinking that because they made those choices, they are at fault for developing an eating disorder. Instead, the eating disorder came first, and the disorder causes people to make what seem like incredibly poor decisions. That doesn't mean people with an eating disorder are powerless, only that the disordered eating is not nearly as simple as a stubborn child who simply refuses to eat.

What you have to begin to separate is that there are behavioral choices that people make. For example, someone can make a behavioral choice to start smoking one cigarette, but by the time the person develops lung disease, the cigarette use has to be treated medically because by then it is a serious illness. You have to stop thinking about all those choices the person made before the lung disease and treat the disease and hopefully help them along so he or she can stop smoking. The disease issue and the choice issue are both important.

Developing Empathy

One of the most important steps in helping children with an eating disorder is learning to treat them with compassion, even if you feel frustrated by their actions. It may be helpful for you to remember to look at eating disorders from a disease perspective. If your child had cancer and was losing hair because of chemotherapy, you probably wouldn't complain about the pieces of hair you had to vacuum off the couch. Well, you wouldn't complain out loud at least.

In Harriet Brown's book, *Brave Girl Eating*, Brown realizes just how difficult the act of eating is for her daughter. She writes, "[My husband] Jamie and I are crying now too, as we understand for the first time exactly how courageous our daughter is. Each time she lifts the spoon to her lips, her whole body shaking, she is jumping out of a plane at thirty thousand feet. Without a parachute."

It's Just Vanity

It's not vanity that drives people with eating disorders to follow extreme diets and obsess over their bodies but a brain disorder that compels the young person to attempt to deal with feelings of shame, anxiety, and powerlessness. That does not mean that wanting to look a certain way isn't involved, but it isn't the primary factor.

She's Craving Attention

When a child has an eating disorder, his or her attention becomes so inwardly focused it is as though no one else exists in the world. People with eating disorders are often seen as selfish and self-absorbed, and they seem to care little for the concerns of those around them or the effect their actions have on others. That being said, it does not mean that a young person's eating disorder has as its goal to get attention. An eating disorder is a real psychological disorder that cannot be turned off and on by the will of the child.

Eating Disorders Aren't That Dangerous

In fact, the mortality rate associated with anorexia nervosa is twelve times higher than the death rate of ALL causes of death for females fifteen to twenty-four years old. All eating disorders can lead to irreversible and even life-threatening health problems, such as heart disease, bone loss, stunted growth, infertility, and kidney damage. Cognitive development is often impacted and can be permanent.

Long-Term Consequences Are Serious

Even though eating disorders are brain disorders, the long-terms effects are both mental and physical. The consequences vary, depending on the type of disordered eating, but what all disordered eating has in common is the long-term damage, from heart and gastrointestinal problems to osteopenia (weakness of the bones) and osteoporosis (brittleness of the bones) to profound growth and development issues and serious dental decay.

Amanda, now twenty-six, has battled bulimia since she was thirteen. She explains, "I have been hospitalized for dehydration many times, have a very hard time with my bowels because of my severe laxative abuse; I have thrown up large amounts of blood, I've passed out, had to get my tonsils out because of the acid eating on them, had to have root canals, I'm always freezing, I bruise so easily, etc. I've also seen my bulimia rip my husband and kids apart!" Amanda received treatment for her bulimia for the first time only last year.

Fatalities Are Real

Fatalities from eating disorders are primarily due to cardiovascular collapse and suicide. Young people can and do die from eating disorders. A study by the National Association of Anorexia Nervosa and Associated Disorders reported that 5–10 percent of anorexics die within ten years after contracting the disease, 18–20 percent of anorexics will be dead after twenty years, and only 30–40 percent ever fully recover. Eating disorders are serious and, without treatment, can lead to long-term physical and emotional problems.

CHAPTER 3

Identifying Signs and Symptoms in Children up to Twelve

E ating disorders are not just for adolescents. Children as young as four are being diagnosed as having binge eating disorder, anorexia, and bulimia. The very early appearance of an eating disorder can make it more difficult to find appropriate treatment, but it's that much more critical to get treatment. Eating disorders have the highest mortality rate of any mental illness, and if you suspect your child may have an eating disorder, the time to act is now.

Children and Disordered Eating

If you have ever spent much time with a child of any age, you'll find that eating issues arise with annoying frequency. Children won't eat food that is a certain color, or they won't eat bread or fruit, or they are simply too busy playing to bother eating. So when is bothersome eating developmentally normal and when is it a sign of something more serious? Early onset eating disorders are those that appear in children younger than thirteen years old. In 2009, the U.S. government published data showing that kids under twelve were the fastest growing population of patients hospitalized for eating disorders.

Fact

The incident rate of restrictive eating disorders in children under the age of twelve is twice that of the incident rate of type 2 diabetes in all children under the age of eighteen. What's interesting is that type 2 diabetes is considered to be an epidemic in children, while eating disorders are referred to as "rare disorders."

Rising Tide

Children have been identified as having an eating disorder as young as four years old, about 3 percent of the total of all people with eating disorders. The Agency for Healthcare Research and Quality found that hospitalizations for eating disorders jumped by 119 percent between 1999 and 2006 for kids younger than twelve. However, it is not clear whether the rise in treatment numbers is due to an increase in cases of eating disorders among children or an increased awareness of the prevalence.

 Essential

The younger the patient group, the more likely that there will be more boys affected by an eating disorder. In children under twelve, the male-female ratio is close to 1:1.

One research study in the United Kingdom indicated the following incidence of eating disorders among children:

- Among children ages six to eight, the incidence is 0.21 per 100,000, rising to 0.92 at ages eight or nine.
- Among children aged nine to ten, the incidence is 1.64, 3.56 at ages ten or eleven, and 4.46 at ages eleven to twelve.
- Among children aged twelve to thirteen, the incidence is 9.51 per 100,000 youngsters.

Research indicates that children who have eating disorders can be roughly divided into three groups. About 40 percent of children have anorexia, 20 percent have binge eating disorder, and 40 percent have another eating disorder, such as bulimia or an eating disorder not otherwise specified.

Shackled to the Scale

"When Alec was seven or eight, he started looking for ways to burn off calories. He would get excused to go to the bathroom at school and he'd do pull-ups in the bathroom for five minutes. The older he got, the more he did. He was always fidgeting. By the time he was eleven, he was running about seven or eight miles, played soccer for two hours, and also worked on his abs every day. Every single day without fail. He gradually started cutting out certain food groups like fats and then carbohydrates. His weight decrease was so slow it took us a long time to notice. By then, his heart was starting to be affected," explained Sara.

Surveys have revealed that one in three girls and a fifth of all boys are concerned about their bodies by ten years old. Children are becoming more and more obsessed with the scale at younger ages.

- 42 percent of girls in first through third grade want to be thinner
- 81 percent of ten-year-olds are afraid of being fat
- 46 percent of nine- to eleven-year-olds are "sometimes" or "very often" on diets

Common Traits

Children who have disordered eating often have very similar characteristics. Typically, such children are described as being:

- Gifted
- Talented
- Perfectionistic

- Anxious
- Sensitive
- Driven or focused
- Competitive

Research shows that almost half of children with early onset eating disorders have a close family member with a history of mental illness. The most common mental health issues include anxiety or depression. Just as with teenagers, children with eating disorders will need treatment beyond refeeding in order to retrain their thinking. Screening and treatment for anxiety, depression, and obsessive-compulsive disorder are all encouraged.

How Do I Know?

If you are concerned about whether your child has an eating disorder, then you have obviously picked up on some physical signs, such as weight loss or gain, emotional signs, or some behaviors that are not typical for your child or that appear to be atypical for children at your child's age and maturity level. Many parents report that their instinct just seemed to tell them something was wrong. However, once you have a feeling that your child has disordered eating, then you need to do your homework and determine if your child's eating patterns need to be addressed.

 Question

How am I supposed to know if my child's eating is normal or not?
The best way to answer that question is to ask if your child's eating is causing physical, emotional, or mental damage. If it isn't, does it have the potential to cause such harm? And remember, questions about eating behaviors can often be addressed by knowledgeable pediatricians.

Picky Eating or Disordered Eating?

What happens when you put a plate full of food in front of your child? Is your child able to eat it or does he push the food around, pick at it, attempt to hide it, or feed it to a family pet? Picky eating may not be an eating disorder, but one in five children who have a diagnosed eating disorder had a history of early feeding problems, such as fussy or fadish eating. Picky eating may be a symptom of an eating disorder, or it may be typical childhood behavior. While you need to pay attention to your child's picky eating, you also need to be able to place it in context of overall behavior and physical changes. The critical difference between a picky eater and a child with an eating disorder is the impact the eating behavior has on a child's physical and mental health. Picky eaters are merely annoying and frustrating, while children with disordered eating have a decreased quality of life because of it.

 Fact

Be aware that 44 percent of children with an eating disorder have a close family member with a history of mental illness, most commonly anxiety or depression.

Other Medical or Psychological Conditions

One of the most important things to do when looking at disordered eating in children is to rule out any other medical or psychological conditions. Eating problems may be indicative of other problems that need medical attention, such as failure to thrive, psychosomatic dwarfism, or oppositional disorder. Existing medical conditions such as prematurity, reactive airway disease, short bowel syndrome, cystic fibrosis, cerebral palsy, developmental delay, autism spectrum disorders, and metabolic disorders can all have a disordered eating component but are not eating disorders as such. For example, the chromosomal disorder *Prader-Willi syndrome* has a *disordered eating* component in terms of an excessive appetite, but it is not a binge eating disorder, though it may share some similarities in behavior.

 Essential

> If your child starts to talk about feeling fat or wanting to change her body size, take time to listen and validate what she is saying. This could be one of the first warning signs you get for an eating disorder.

Whether or not eating irregularities can be considered disordered eating lies in the fact that the child has become inflexible and refuses to consider change, not only with food, but with other areas of life as well. Be aware that obsessive-compulsive behaviors in children that show themselves through eating are commonly misconstrued as eating disorders.

Disordered Eating Conditions in Children

Anorexia nervosa, bulimia nervosa, and binge eating disorder are the most common eating disorders seen in children. Other forms of disordered eating that may show up in children are:

- Pervasive refusal syndrome, which is characterized by refusal to eat, drink, walk, talk, or care for themselves in any way over a period of months.
- Appetite loss due to depression.
- Functional dysphagia: fear of vomiting, swallowing, or choking that often begins after an adverse event.
- Selective eating. The child limits food intake to a very narrow range of preferred foods. Weight is typically not adversely affected, although growth may be.
- Pica, or the eating of nonfood items, such as clay, paper, coins or other nonedible items.

Physical Signs

Sometimes the easiest way to tell if a child has an eating disorder is to look for characteristic weight gain or loss. However, in its earliest stages, there may be no weight change at all. These are the physical signs that may be present with anorexia and in some cases with bulimia:

- Feeling cold all the time
- Dry skin
- Puffy face
- Fine hair on body
- Thinning of hair on head; dry and brittle hair
- Muscle weakness
- Yellow skin
- Cold, mottled hands and feet or swelling of feet

Remember that some eating disorders, such as binge eating disorder, may not be evident physically as the child may be of a normal weight. In the absence of physical symptoms, parents will need to identify and track specific disordered eating behaviors.

 Fact

The American Academy of Pediatrics recommends that all preteens should be screened for eating disorders at their regular checkups because of the growing incidence of the problem, especially among boys and minorities.

Weight Loss

Ever since your child was an infant, your child's weight and height have been measured. In fact, it's one of the first things to be done in the delivery room, after announcing whether it's a boy or a girl. Some babies are born small and stay relatively petite all of their lives. If Mom and Dad are both on the small side, their son or daughter might well follow in their footsteps, and conversely, if Mom and Dad are both big-boned, it's possible that their offspring will follow suit. That being said, you can't simply look at your child's weight on one day and determine if she weighs too much, too little, or could have an eating disorder. You have to find a way to bring some perspective to that number. First of all, is your child's weight significantly higher or lower than the last time she went to the doctor's office? If you don't know, call and ask the office for the last several weigh-in dates and the recorded weights.

Another way of understanding the number is to look at the child's BMI. A child's BMI is calculated using the child's height, weight, gender, and birth date. A child's BMI-for-age calculator can be found on the Centers for Disease Control website at *http://apps.nccd.cdc.gov/dnpabmi/.* You can use this calculator for children and teens, ages two through nineteen years old. In adults, the results are simple to understand because the BMI corresponds to a certain weight classification. In children, the numbers are used differently. Instead, a BMI-for-age percentile chart is used, and you plot what percentile a child is in to see what the corresponding classification is. For children, the CDC breaks it down as following:

Percentile	Weight Status
Less than 5th	Underweight
5th–84th	Healthy
85th–94th	Overweight
95th and above	Obese

To see the CDC's BMI-for-age percentile chart, go to *http://apps .nccd.cdc.gov/dnpabmi/Images/growthchart_example1.gif.* The BMI-for-age percentile is one tool that can be useful, but it must be understood in relationship to your particular child's weight patterns.

 **Essential**

Weight Gain

Not all children who are overweight have binge eating disorder, but most children who binge eat are overweight. The incidence of binge eating disorder rises with age, and the earliest signs
often begin with puberty, typically around age twelve. However,
binge eating disorder can appear in younger children. Research
has shown children with binge eating disorder describe feeling a
loss of control around food and reported more anxiety, depressive
symptoms, negative moods, and body dissatisfaction than children
with no loss of control. In addition, children who reported loss of
control over eating also were more likely to endorse that weight
and shape played an important role in self-evaluation. A history of
dieting in children has not been shown to increase the likelihood
of developing binge eating disorder. Signs that a child has binge
eating disorder are often different from those for adolescents and
adults. They include:

- Recurrent episodes of binge eating. An episode of binge eating is characterized by both of the following:

  1. Food seeking in the absence of hunger (e.g., after a full
     meal)
  2. A sense of lack of control over eating (e.g., endorse
     that, "When I start to eat, I just can't stop")

- Binge episodes are associated with one or more of the
  following:

1. Food seeking in response to negative affect (e.g., sadness, boredom, restlessness)
2. Food seeking as a reward
3. Sneaking or hiding food

- Symptoms persist over a period of three months
- Eating is not associated with the regular use of inappropriate compensatory behaviors (e.g., purging, fasting, excessive exercise) and does not occur exclusively during the course of anorexia nervosa or bulimia nervosa. Consistently self-reported ingestion of large amounts of food is not characteristic of binge eating disorder in children, but it is universal in teens and adults with binge eating disorder.

Emotional Signs

When a child who may be overweight loses weight, a child without an eating disorder may be happy, but a child with an eating disorder still wants to lose more. When an overweight child loses weight, his social life grows, whereas it tends to decrease in a child with an eating disorder. A child with an eating disorder may become socially isolated from friends and peers for several reasons, including a sense of inferiority or an attempt to keep feelings of hurt and anger buried, or a desire to keep their disordered eating a secret. A typical child's self-esteem grows, while a child with disordered eating will have decreased self-esteem because whatever weight is lost isn't enough, or their self-hatred grows because of certain behaviors, such as binging. Self-induced vomiting is only found in a child with disordered eating.

Where's My Kid?

One of the first signs of an eating disorder is that the child begins to withdraw emotionally. That can be difficult to differentiate between the separating process that many middle school students go through en route to adolescence.

Steve, whose son, Carl, began his eating disorder in middle school, describes the changes that he first began seeing. "Carl has always been an open book. Usually within the first few minutes of meeting him, you'll know everything about him. He'll tell you everything that's going on in his life. About halfway through fifth grade, he started talking less. He started staying home more. He started becoming I wouldn't say moody, but not as outgoing as he once was." Those personality changes were the first signs of his eating disorder.

 Essential

Remember that you are not to blame for your child's disordered eating. In fact, millions of dollars and decades of effort have been spent on countless research studies and not a single eating disorder researcher has been able to identify a single thing that parents do not do, or do, that causes disordered eating in their children.

Altered Sense of Self

"I can remember being eight years old and standing in front of my mirror and just crying. I remember hating the way I looked. My twin sister and I were in the same classes and someone said the way they could tell us apart was that I was the chubby one. A few kids picked it up and 'Chubs' became my new nickname. I was only in third grade and I hated my thighs, my stomach, even my bottom. When I look back on my life, I think of it as before the day I got called Chubs and afterward."

A child with an eating disorder will typically have an altered sense of self—that is, any perceived flaws are seen as overwhelming and huge. In the above example, when Sarah looks back, she realized she probably only weighed five or ten pounds more than her sister, but the difference seemed enormous. She perceived her body to be much larger than it actually was.

Unhealthy Behaviors

Even if your child's weight has not fluctuated, and you aren't seeing any specific emotional changes, you may be able to identify disordered eating by looking for several different behaviors that would be unusual for your child, such as:

- Following a highly restrictive diet
- Skipping meals
- Consistently going to the restroom immediately following meals
- Exercising an excessive amount
- Becoming excessively concerned about appearance, weight, and/or body size
- Making disparaging comments about other people because of their weight, size, or appearance

Special Considerations for Treatment

Once you decide that your child may well have disordered eating, then you have to make the next right step, which typically involves finding the right treatment team. As you will no doubt soon learn, eating disorder resources for children are more difficult to find than those for adolescents and young adults.

Research for early onset eating disorders lags behind treatment for teens and adult, but early research and anecdotal reports suggest that family-based treatment is an appropriate treatment option for children with disordered eating. "My eleven-year-old daughter is just coming out of a battle with anorexia. She was in serious condition —extremely thin, a heart rate of 42, and dangerously low blood pressure. I was amazed at the quick progression of the disease from the time we suspected something to the time she was noticeably sick. I so thankful that we were directed to an eating disorder center that guided us through family-based therapy. In a matter of six months, my daughter has gone from a total repulsion of food to eating on her own and with pleasure. We proceed with caution, but we are amazed at how well this treatment has worked for my daughter and for me, her major caregiver through this illness. For younger anorexics, I think the form of treatment can work wonders."

Hospitalization

While there is not a significant amount of research available on treating children with eating disorders, preliminary studies found that half of the children diagnosed with an eating disorder needed to be admitted to the hospital. One year after diagnosis, 73 percent had improved, 6 percent were worse, and 10 percent were unchanged. It may be better for a child who needs to be hospitalized to be placed on a regular pediatric unit and not the psychiatric unit, as the psychiatric unit maybe overwhelming for young children, especially if children and teens are placed in the same unit.

 Fact

It is completely possible for children with disordered eating to experience being physically healthy, mentally healthy, and no longer having any of the distortions or eating disorder thoughts. Complete recovery is the most common outcome when treating children. This is most likely because younger patients tend to recover more readily than patients who have had eating disorders for a number of years.

Finding Appropriate Professionals

Marc A. Zimmer, PhD, explains that "treatment needs to be with a truly experienced child or adolescent professional with many years of working with this special population. A generalist is not adequate and could potentially be destructive."

There are a number of residential treatment programs for children, but because there are fewer options than for older children, you may be placed in a position where you need to have her hospitalized far away from home, where frequent visiting may be difficult. However, keep in mind that family therapy is considered a key to successful treatment of eating disorders, even with children, and it is very important to be able to participate regularly in such therapy sessions.

Accept the Process

Treating children with eating disorders is going to be complicated and may well take longer to treat than adolescents. Dr. Zimmer explains, "With those patients who are under thirteen, many are embarrassed or not as verbal or descriptive as older patients. Therefore, usually more patience is needed. Medications are usually less frequently prescribed, but certainly, if indicated, they might be prescribed. At times, special treatment modalities are needed. For example, art therapy, dance movement therapy, music therapy, etc."

Children and Medication

There is no eating disorder pill. While medications may be effective in treating your child's eating disorder, there are few long-term studies that support one pharmacological approach over another. While your primary care physician may be willing to prescribe a psychotropic medication, this is one time when you need to find an experienced psychiatrist who can not only prescribe the correct medication but can monitor your child for the long term. Above all, you should seek a psychiatrist who expects to follow your child over time and who requires office visits and follow-up telephone calls whenever a new medication is prescribed or a medication dose is changed. Initially, follow-up may be in one to three weeks, with monthly office visits going onward. However, this depends on the nature of the symptoms, the type of medication, and whether the medication is working or not. Some prescription medications require initial blood testing, then again if the dose is changed, and at specific intervals thereafter, such as every three to six months.

 **Essential**

As parents, you can help the first psychiatrist's appointments go more smoothly by coming prepared with written information that includes significant life events with approximate dates, medication history, and the patient's behavioral, medical, as well as family history.

Differences Between Children and Teens

It is important to note that children have less body fat than their adolescent counterparts and, consequently, become skeletal more rapidly. Many physicians and researchers argue that because of the differences in body composition, a 15 percent weight loss, rather than the usual 25 percent, should be a criterion for the diagnosis of childhood onset anorexia. Anorexia in childhood can cause multiple problems, including delaying puberty, growth, and breast development.

Prevention

The single best recommended strategy to help your child avoid developing an eating disorder is to avoid placing them on a diet. Dieting is recognized as a powerful risk factor for eating disorders. Instead, it is more effective and healthier to focus on healthy eating, choosing healthy physical activity, and a healthy lifestyle, discussed and modeled in a way that does not belittle, discourage, or threaten self-esteem.

Top Prevention Tips

It is impossible to completely prevent early onset eating disorders, but you can take active steps to reduce the likelihood that they will emerge. Some suggestions:

- Never skip meals.
- Offer healthy foods in your home.
- Eat with your child.
- Make fun exercise a part of your weekly parent-child routine.
- Deal with your own attitudes about weight, eating, and body image.
- Never criticize your child's shape or weight or allow criticisms of others' appearances.
- Help your child develop his or her communication skills, especially about feelings.

Can't Beat Genetics

There is a strong genetic component in eating disorders, but that doesn't mean you can't take steps to decrease the likelihood that your child may develop an eating disorder. This may mean speaking to your pediatrician about regular screenings, declaring your home a diet-free zone, and understanding your child's risk factors for food and size issues. Talk to your child, as appropriate developmentally, about values and healthy thinking habits. Plus, you can be an excellent role model of how to cope with stressors. Whether you take yoga, journal, go for a walk, or have a good cry, teaching your children how to deal with difficult feelings is an important part of parenting a healthy young person.

CHAPTER 4

Identifying Signs and Symptoms in Adolescents and Young Adults

E ating disorders are the third most common chronic disease among teenage girls, up to one in ten of whom will die from it. Adolescents and young adults aren't the only ones who suffer, but a person who has an eating disorder will be most likely to develop symptoms during this period. Characterized by a preoccupation with food and a distortion of body image, adolescents and teens need comprehensive treatment to be relieved of the symptoms.

How to Tell If Your Child Has an Eating Disorder

Parents aren't the only ones who have difficulty identifying and diagnosing eating disorders (EDs), especially in young children and adolescents. Eating disorders, says Dr. Mark Zimmer, "are called 'The Secretive Disorder.' Often, for prolonged periods of time, they appear to be normal patterns of eating. As the disorder progresses the symptoms become more apparent. Patients feel that the eating disorder is totally under their control. Oftentimes, it takes a medical or psychological emergency for the eating disorder to be discovered."

Innocent Beginnings

There are some people who go into a normal weight loss program who receive positive reinforcement and ego gratification from friends and family. "Over a period of time," explains Zimmer, "some of those people, who have predisposing factors, become obsessive with the weight loss. The time frame can be rapid or slow, depending upon the individual and how predisposed they are to the situation. In other words, what starts as a normal weight loss program can sometimes end up to be the onset of an ED."

Secrecy as a Symptom

If your child has a fever or a rash, you can tell. You can measure it. You can identify the problem neatly and specifically. It can be frustrating for parents, who have spent years dealing with childhood illnesses, to try to clarify if an eating disorder exists. If you have a checklist of behaviors and you can see whether or not your child meets those criteria, it would be easy. Part of what makes it hard is that if you ask your child specific questions about his or her behaviors, thinking habits, and even physical symptoms, you aren't likely to get an honest answer. Plus, not only will adolescents and young adults often hide the extent of the problem, they will often need to hide the related behaviors, such as lying and stealing.

As Genifer, a former anorexic explains, "When I turned sixteen, I got my first job at a beauty supply store. We sold professional-grade hair dyes, perms, blow dryers, etc. I learned that we also sold diet pills and diuretics. Around the six month of working there, right before we closed, I stole three boxes of each. My breakfast of Trix and skim milk got replaced with two diet pills, two diuretics, and a vitamin, all washed down with no-sugar-added cranberry juice. I lost twenty pounds in three weeks. I stopped adding mayonnaise to my tuna salad. I stopped eating anything for lunch, even on the weekends, when my grandmother continuously asked me to let her cook something for me. I then stopped eating anything for dinner, telling my grandmother that I ate at work."

Signs and Symptoms of an Eating Disorder

Children who have an eating disorder may have certain characteristics, such as perfectionism and having a low self-esteem. Specific behaviors that may indicate an eating disorder include:

- Drastic weight loss in a short period of time
- Total elimination of a food group (or groups)
- Becoming a vegetarian
- Complaints of food allergies, etc.
- Inability to break rigid routines (especially food and exercise patterns)
- Difficulty concentrating
- Denial of disorder
- Mood swings
- Difficulty asking for help
- Skipping meals
- Exercising obsessively
- Becoming overly concerned about appearance, weight, and body size
- Making disparaging comments about others because of their weight or size

Signs and Symptoms of Anorexia Nervosa

According to the National Institute of Mental Health, physical consequences that might be seen in a young person with anorexia include:

- Thinning of the bones (osteopenia or osteoporosis)
- Brittle hair and nails
- Dry and yellowish skin
- Growth of fine hair over body (lanugo)
- Mild anemia, and muscle weakness and loss

- Severe constipation
- Low blood pressure, slowed breathing and pulse
- Drop in internal body temperature, causing a person to feel cold all the time
- Lethargy

Signs and Symptoms of Bulimia

When a young person with bulimia binges, the amount of food he or she can eat is incredible. They can eat more than most adults can eat in a few days. It isn't unusual to come home after an absence or to wake up in the morning and find that a significant amount of food in the home is just gone.

"I have bulimia and when I am in the midst of a binge, I can't even describe how good food tastes. There's no way to describe how explosive all the flavors are. When my stomach fills up to the point where I can't eat another bite, then it's like 'Oh no,' and it's an explosion. When I finish purging, it's like a different thing altogether. There's this frantic, 'I have to get this out of me now, now, now.' It's a different euphoria and it feels good because it's all gone. I don't know anymore what it feels like to eat a normal meal and keep it down."

Signs and symptoms that you see in a young person with bulimia include:

- Sudden, rapid consumption of large quantities of food
- Regularly going into the bathroom immediately after a meal
- Using laxatives, diuretics, or enemas after meals
- Smell of vomit on the person or in the bathroom
- Excessive exercising or use of sauna
- Calluses or scarring on the knuckles or hands from using fingers to induce vomiting
- Puffy or "chipmunk" cheeks caused by repeated vomiting
- Discolored teeth that may be yellow, ragged, or clear from exposure to stomach acid when throwing up

- Normal weight or may be slightly overweight. Being under-weight and purging may indicate a purging type of anorexia.
- Frequent weight fluctuations

Many teens will learn to hide their purging by playing music to cover up the sound, or even do so in their bedroom in a plastic container. They may also purge in the shower as it covers up the noise and makes less mess.

 Fact

When your child leaves the bathroom, pay attention if he starts using air freshener every time or is suddenly making sure he is carrying chewing gum or breath mints to cover up bad breath.

Signs and Symptoms of Binge Eating Disorder

"I knew my daughter was overweight. It was obvious. Anyone who looked at her could see it. But what I didn't realize was that she really had a problem beyond just eating too much. She had a real disease that needed treatment. We had waited a long time before we started taking her binge eating seriously, and I wish we hadn't waited so long," says Suzanne, whose daughter is now in treatment for binge eating disorder.

The signs of binge eating disorder are:

- Eating large amounts of food
- Eating a large quantity, even when child is full
- Eating rapidly during binge episodes
- Eating behavior that seems to be out of control
- Frequent dieting, possibly without weight loss
- Frequently eating alone
- Being depressed, disgusted, or upset about eating
- Weight may be average or overweight

Is Vegetarianism an Eating Disorder?

According to New Hampshire eating disorder specialist and nutrition counselor Marcia Herrin, EdD, MPH, RD, LD, author of *Nutritional Counseling in the Treatment of Eating Disorders*, vegetarianism is common among eating disorder patients. Teenagers and young adults, ages fifteen to twenty-three, who report they are vegetarian are more likely at some point to engage in unhealthy weight-loss behaviors like binging, purging, and using diet pills or laxatives, according to a study by The *Journal of the American Dietetic Association* in 2009.

"Adolescents may use vegetarianism to express independence from their families, which is very common at this age," Herrin explains. "However, teenagers may also be using this form of more restrictive eating as a cover for reducing fat and caloric intake, which can then lead to both disordered eating and eating disorders."

Elizabeth, who started disordered eating at fourteen, agrees. "After I had been 'found out,' I decided I would become a vegetarian. Refusing to eat any meat, which was another way of control, of course this was because the doctors had caught on and were threatening to lock me up if I didn't start eating."

If your child has become a vegetarian, don't automatically assume that an eating disorder is present. Do, however, look deeper. Ask why your child is a vegetarian. Look at the meals she is eating. Are they balanced? Do they provide enough nutrition and calories to sustain a healthy life?

Obsessive Behavior

A young person with an eating disorder will think a lot about food, regardless of the type of eating disorder. That obsession may be evident in these behaviors

- Counting calories
- Taking small bites

- Cutting food into very small pieces
- Hiding food under other pieces of food
- Drinking a lot of water between bites of food
- Shrouding food, or ruining food on one's plate by pouring salt or water on it

Ironically, or perhaps as a way of coping with self-starvation, the young person will often find ways to surround herself with food, whether by cooking or serving food to friends and family members.

Obsession with Food

Many children and teenagers with an eating disorder will obsess about food, regardless of the type of eating disorder they have. A child who is a compulsive overeater may hoard food, think about food, and even plan the next day's menu before going to sleep the next day. What is particularly ironic is that even young people who are anorexic focus—even obsessively—on food. Juliet, for example, who has had anorexia since age eleven, is not unusual in her almost perverse fascination with food and cooking. She bakes every day and makes a lavish meal for her parents every night, never even tasting it. It is also a safe way to be near food without getting fat. Cooking may be a way of feeling safe by engaging in "normal" behavior. Cooking magazines or television shows may also be a focus.

Obsession with Numbers

Often, someone with disordered eating isn't just focused on food, he or she is also focused on numbers. The scale, of course, is the primary culprit, with affected children and teens weighing themselves up to a dozen times a day or more. Dress size, bra size, calorie counting, waist, hip, and arm measurements, even the amount of calories burned by each minute of exercise—these all compete for space in the mind of someone with disordered eating. In a very real way, they become trapped inside this sinister world where numbers are literally life and death. "Do I weigh less today than I did yesterday?" "How many calories did I just eat?" "I climbed twenty-seven steps thirty-four times—that should make up for the quarter of the muffin I ate this morning."

Physical Signs

You may have seen the stick-thin pictures of anorexic young women and wonder how it would be possible not to know if your child has an eating disorder. Realize that many people with bulimia are at an average weight, and it can take months or even years of food restriction before an anorexic has the extremely thin look.

Look for these signs and symptoms:

- Feeling cold all the time
- Sleep problems
- Cuts and calluses across the top of finger joints (from sticking finger down throat to cause vomiting)
- Dry skin
- Puffy face
- Fine hair on body
- Thinning of hair on head, dry and brittle hair
- Cavities or discoloration of teeth from vomiting
- Muscle weakness
- Yellow skin
- Cold, mottled hands and feet or swelling of feet
- Missing at least three periods in a row (amenorrhea)

Weight

You cannot determine if your child has an eating disorder based on your child's current weight, unless your teen is severely underweight or overweight. If you suspect your child has an eating disorder, get rid of the scale, or at least keep it under lock and key. Being able to track weight is an important piece of a child's eating disorder, particularly for anorexia. Not being able to know exactly what he weighs can be uncomfortable for someone with an eating disorder, as it can make him feel out of control. When you weigh your child, ask him to turn around and cover the numbers on the scale. When you are done, hide the scale. If your child doesn't have access to the scale, he can focus less on the numbers. It isn't unusual for a teen with an eating disorder to weigh himself multiple times a day and to keep a journal tracking weight, measurements, and food intake.

Alert

If you've decided to ditch the scale, watch out for your Wii. Popular games like Wii Fit maintain records of your weight and can track your progress over weeks and months. Each person's Wii Fit account is password protected, so you'll need to carefully monitor your child's use to see if she is using the Wii Fit board as a makeshift scale.

How to Use the BMI

As was discussed in Chapter 3, the CDC uses a BMI-for-age percentile chart for children ages two to nineteen (*http://apps.nccd .cdc.gov/dnpabmi/*). For young adults over the age of nineteen, the adult BMI chart is used, in which a particular BMI (using just height and weight) corresponds to a classification (see the following table).

BMI	Weight Status
Below 18.5	Underweight
18.5–24.9	Normal
25.0–29.9	Overweight
30.0 and above	Obese

Again, the BMI number is just one measurement, and it must be understood in relationship to your particular child's weight patterns.

Scale Tricks

As anyone who has ever tried to lose weight knows, there are certain strategies you can use in an attempt to "trick" the scale. If you want to weigh less, you use the restroom first, wear less clothing, and don't eat anything beforehand. In the same way, children, especially adolescents, who are trying to lose weight and keep parental units off their back have come up with a number of tricks to artificially inflate the numbers on the scale.

Your child may attempt to trick the scale (and you) by:

- Drinking lots of water before weighing
- Wearing heavy shoes
- Wearing jeans and multiple layers of clothing
- Adding small weights or coins to hems, pockets, bra, or hair scrunchie
- Avoiding having a bowel movement

 Alert

With information like how to trick the scale, you may decide it isn't appropriate to leave this book out so your child can read it. On the other hand, if your child knows you know her tricks, she may be less likely to try them.

Emotional Signs

While an eating disorder is a disease that affects your child's body, his or her emotions are not exempt. One of the hallmarks of an eating disorder is feeling as though you are living on an emotional roller coaster with your child. Her emotions may swing wildly, depending on what the scale says, on what she ate, on how she thinks her thighs look, or for some other reason even she can't identify.

"I feel helpless to help. I don't know what to do. My biggest fear is that I am going to lose my child. This will kill her if she doesn't stop. Our daughter used to be loving and caring, but not anymore. It has wrapped itself around her soul. She has changed—her entire focus is on food and not eating and cooking and calories and exercise, and she doesn't seem to care about anyone or anything else. She's not very likeable right now. This isn't my daughter and I want her back."

Power and Control

"One day you realize that the child with the eating disorder has somehow taken over control of the family. It was shocking for me to realize the number of decisions that (my daughter) was making for the family—what we ate, what restaurants we eat at, what gets served for birthdays and holidays, even what we put in the refrigerator. She will cover it up, and sometimes she'll just throw it out if she doesn't want to see it. That's after she asks me questions about why I bought it in the first place and what am I trying to do to her. It is exhausting," says Shannon, whose daughter has been bulimic for three years.

It's not about the food. It seems as though it is about the food, since every discussion and argument is about food, and so much attention is paid to what gets eaten when, but it isn't the food that's the problem. A parent could be a gourmet chef or a have every food delivery number on speed dial and it wouldn't make a difference to a child with an eating disorder. It isn't about what's being served, how much is being served, or how it's presented. Food is just the manifestation of the problem.

Isolation

A child with an eating disorder rarely chooses to spend much time interacting in a healthy way with others. Many times they will excuse themselves from activities that they once enjoyed, especially time with family. Your child may choose to spend a significant amount of time alone in their room. Plus, they may refuse to attend social events because so many of them involve food and are particularly anxiety-provoking.

Elizabeth describes the beginnings of her eating disorder as a sense of loneliness. "As a teen, we all experience the basic feelings of being lost out in the world, not really knowing or understanding, feeling totally alone out there or misunderstood. . . . . My dealings with food those years were a basic means of control, a way to deal with those feelings the only way I knew how. Sometimes I would eat, sometimes I wouldn't.

"I just wanted to be alone with my eating disorder. I can go to my happy place and don't have to deal with life, with my future, with anything."

It's a Thinking Problem

The way your child acts is based on the way she is thinking. If the thinking is flawed, then the feelings will follow. Here is one teenager in the throes of an eating disorder: "I don't binge, or purge, or even exercise. I simply only eat when I'm hungry. Granted, I began killing the 'hunger signal' when I was a little kid, so it's easy to control now. There is no damage to my body . . . yet? And I think bones are beautiful. I hate the fact that I have skin over them even. So what if I die early? I will have lived nearly forty years thin, and I will die thin. I don't care if anyone thinks it's a disorder. It's just self-discipline and everyone else is just jealous," explains Polly, at eighteen, who has had an eating disorder for four years. Because the thinking is flawed, it is a mental disorder with a medical component. Changing the thinking is a critical component in successful treatment. This is one reason that cognitive behavioral therapy, or CBT, is so successful in children and adults with disordered eating. Cognitive behavioral therapy focuses on changing the thinking, which changes the emotions, which can then change what your child says and does.

Watch the Response

What happens if all the scales in the house are gone one day? How does your child respond when a high-calorie meal is placed in front of him? How does she react if she can't get access to a restroom for an hour after a meal? Sometimes the most useful information is gleaned simply by watching what your child does when forced to confront his or her disordered eating habits. In fact, test meals can be used in a number of ways in treatment planning and evaluation. For example, a meal that consists of standard servings from each of the food groups may be administered, and the amount of each food and overall calories consumed can be observed. How does your teen respond? Is there hesitancy? Can the child eat without difficulty or without purging?

Misperception

When a young person has an eating disorder, it is common to have a misperception of what his or her body looks like. Amy, for example, at 5'5" weighed 92 pounds and would stand in front of her mirror and write down in her journal all of the things she hated about her body. One day's entry reads, "I see fat in places I do not want it to be there. I definitely see a lot of fat over here on my thighs. My face is swollen here. I look huge. I am so fat and so ugly."

Misperception is especially true for anorexia and bulimia, and less true for other eating disorders. However, children with other eating disorders may be very self-critical about their bodies.

Unhealthy Coping Strategies

Living with an eating disorder is agonizing and painful. As such, many young people will turn to other coping mechanisms such as self-injury, gambling, or shoplifting. A number of those with eating disorders will turn to substance abuse to cope with their eating disorder. "The first indication of my daughter's eating disorder was her cutting. I took her to a counselor to get help, but only then did her restricted eating come out. I had no idea. But only by treating the first could we get to the truth," says one mom.

Remember that many young people have a coexisting mental health issue such as depression or anxiety, and substance abuse can be a dangerous but temporarily effective means of self-medicating. Research indicates that up to half of adolescents and young adults with eating disorders will use alcohol or drugs, in comparison to only 9 percent of those without an eating disorder. Looking at the problem from another perspective, up to a third of alcohol or illicit drug abusers have eating disorders, compared to 3 percent of the general population.

Concurrent Drug Use

Caffeine, laxatives, and diuretics are the most commonly abused drugs of choice for those with eating disorders. Amphetamines, barbiturates, tranquilizers, cocaine, and heroin are often used initially as a way to suppress appetite, increase metabolism, and purge unwanted calories. They have the added "bonus" of self-medicating negative emotions. The use of any of these substances can lead to physical dependence and even addiction.

The types of drugs used tend to vary by eating disorder. For example, if a young person is anorexic, amphetamines are the most common drug of choice. The perceived benefits of amphetamines, which are stimulants, include increased metabolism rate and decreased appetite. Anorexics are more likely to avoid alcohol use because of the number of calories in alcohol and the lack of control when drinking. In the same way, marijuana tends to increase the appetite and is likely to be avoided. Those who purge are more likely to crave the sedative effects of tranquilizers and alcohol. Cocaine and cigarettes are often more common with those with anorexia.

Adding a chemical addiction on top of an eating disorder obviously creates even more barriers to diagnosis and treatment. Drug and alcohol use may provide temporary relief for the psychological pain, but it merely exacerbates feelings of being powerless and out of control. In addition, it does more damage to the person's physical health.

Concurrent Self-Injury

Self-inflicted bodily harm or self-mutilation can often accompany eating disorders. It can be difficult to exactly determine what self-injury is, but it is most commonly associated with intentional burning, ripping or pulling skin or hair, cutting of the skin, or carving, scratching, or even breaking bones. Sometimes even excessive piercing and tattooing can be included.

It can be very difficult for parents and others to understand the motive behind self-injury. The paradox is that, with self-injury, most sufferers explain that they do it in order to just feel something or to relieve emotional pain. Many people who self-injure report feeling either emotional numbness or overwhelming sadness or anxiety. As with an eating disorder, those who engage in self-injurious behavior may do so to feel in control of their bodies and minds.

The Risk of Athletics

Participating in athletics promotes physical conditioning and sets a foundation for enjoying a lifetime of physical activity. Children of all ages can learn teamwork and build self-esteem. Athletic competition can also be stressful, and when combined with other factors, especially in someone predisposed to having disordered eating, then eating disorders may develop.

Male and female athletes are especially at risk for eating disorders, especially those who compete in weight-class sports like boxing, wrestling, and crew and those who participate in aesthetic sports like diving, swimming, and gymnastics. Research among Division 1 NCAA athletes found that a third of female athletes were at risk for disordered eating.

There are several risk factors for athletics-related eating disorders:

- Pressure to win from parents and coaches
- Too much criticism, not enough praise
- Emphasis on appearance/weight
- Critical of their own athletic performance

Signs and Symptoms

Athletes suffering from an eating disorder may show signs of the following physiological conditions, including:

- Fatigue
- Overuse injuries
- Dehydration
- Training more than trainer recommends
- Training without enjoyment
- Training when sick or in dangerous situations (e.g., alone at night)
- Loss of speed, coordination, and endurance
- Muscle cramps
- Menstrual irregularities

Female Athlete Triad

Female athlete triad is a serious health concern that has been identified among athletes, particularly girls and women who participate in competitive sports. The criteria include a combination of disordered eating (or low energy availability or energy deficiency—"underfueling"), amenorrhea (abnormal or missing periods), and osteoporosis (weak bones). The long-term health risks for the female athlete triad can be serious. The lack of good bone health as a teenager means an increased likelihood of bone problems later in life. Plus, irregular or missed periods can make it more difficult to become pregnant or maintain a healthy pregnancy and have children.

Fact

Weight-Class Sports

Your fourteen-year-old son is a wrestler who has been trying to make the 100-pound weight category for a competition next week. He is 5 feet 3 inches, and his coach has told him that someday he could go to the Olympics. He checks the scale every few hours and is frustrated that his weight is holding at 105 pounds. He is eating 500 calories a day and carrying around a container that he spits in. You know how important this is to him, and, though you're worried, this is just for a few weeks. How bad can it be?

While some children can encounter this pressure for a few weeks and come out unscathed, if your son has a predisposition toward having an eating disorder, this is the kind of situation that can trigger it. As such, this is a dangerous routine to get into and it can have serious consequences.

In weight-class sports like boxing, wrestling, and crew, team members have to make weight or maintain a certain body size in order to stay competitive.

 Essential

Aesthetic Sports

In sports like figure skating, gymnastics, and ballet, the emphasis is focused less on the team and more on individual appearance.

Natasha Friend, author of *Perfect*, a novel on eating disorders for middle schoolers, drew on her own experience as a young gymnast in writing her book. "As a gymnast I was introduced to the concept of dieting and weight control at an early age. Our coach labeled the two springboards in our gym with tape and magic marker: "Under 100 Pounds" and "Over 100 Pounds." There was no question about which board was acceptable and which wasn't. I went on my first diet at the age of eleven—and I wasn't even overweight. I never developed a full-blown eating disorder, but I knew girls who did, and I certainly dabbled in some of the behavior: laxatives (once was enough), binge eating, and vomiting."

 Alert

Gymnast Christy Henrich is one of the more well-known fatalities from eating disorders. Christy was told by a judge that she had to lose weight in order to make the Olympic team. She did so but died of multiple organ failure, as a result of anorexia, at the age of twenty-two, weighing only sixty pounds.

College Concerns

Stress can trigger an eating disorder, and even positive changes can be stressful. Going away to college for the first time, or even starting college while living at home, is often a very stressful event in the lives of young men and women. College students can be vulnerable to weight gain and disordered eating, often at the same time. Students not only have increased autonomy over their meals, often for the first time, but they often have busy schedules that may make not eating far too easy.

Eating Disorder Prevalence in College

Many young people develop eating disorders during their college years. In fact, 86 percent of people with eating disorders develop them around the age of twenty. As many as 10 percent of college women suffer from a clinical, or nearly clinical, eating disorder, which includes 5.1 percent who suffer from bulimia nervosa. According to the American College Health Association's annual survey, in only a decade, the number of college students dieting, vomiting, or taking laxatives to lose weight has jumped from about 28 to 38 percent.

 Fact

Most colleges have a counseling center that offers initial assessments, group therapy, short-term individual counseling, psychiatric services (for students who might benefit from medication), and assistance with referrals for long-term and specialty services. Staff members can usually consult with family and friends about how to proceed to encourage a student to come for help, though they may be bound by confidentiality rules.

Specific College Risks

Separating from family and living in a dorm or being closely connected to other young people who may watch them more closely may set up a young person who may be predisposed to an eating disorder. If they lose weight, students may receive positive attention, which can further reinforce their interest in losing more weight. For some students who are vulnerable, the mind-set of dieting can be the trigger for beginning an eating disorder. Laxatives, vomiting, and excessive exercising can become a vicious and increasingly entrenched cycle that can have devastating consequences.

Do Your Research

How much privacy does a teenager need? The easy answer? Not as much as the teenager wants. Your teenager is still your child, and sometimes the best way to find out accurate information about what is happening with your child is to snoop. Kim Moore, a child advocate and cognitive behavioral accountability trainer with twenty-three years' experience explains, "Privacy is not something a child is entitled to. It is the parent's responsibility to know what is going on with their child. Especially when there is reason for concern, finding out what you can is your responsibility. The immoral thing to do is turn your head and refuse to face the problem head-on. Your child's right to privacy does not supersede their right to be safe and happy. When your child is in danger it is our moral obligation to protect them, not only from the world, but from themselves. Entering a child's room and going through drawers, and reading texts and e-mails and journals gives you the information you need to help you make the kinds of decisions your child needs you to make so they can become healthy and happy adults. If we give that obligation up and take the responsibility on, then we're setting them up for more pain."

Items that might indicate disordered eating include:

- Excessive food wrappers from binging
- Hidden toothbrushes used for inducing vomiting
- Laxatives (pills, powders, suppositories, or teas), diuretics (water pills), or weight-loss pills
- Syrup of ipecac or other medications to induce vomiting
- Enemas
- Notebooks with drawings or photographs of very thin models
- Razor blades or other items used to cut
- Diary with self-reporting of disordered eating, daily calorie intake, or body measurements

- Participation on online pro–eating disorder sites
- Drugs or drug paraphernalia

Keep in mind that there is a good possibility that your child has intentionally, or at least subconsciously, left something out for you to find. Your child may not know any other way of broaching the subject with you and will know that if you see something incriminating, then you will bring it up to him. Leaving it out is a way to open the doors of communication with you.

Ask

Sit down and talk. Talk about the behaviors you've seen and why you're concerned.

Don't expect your child with an eating disorder to be honest. In fact, you are better off if you prepare yourself for the fact that your child will lie about having an eating disorder, about the severity of the eating disorder, and about the specifics. It is fine for the conversation to end with you disagreeing with your child about what the next steps should be. As the parent, you are responsible for being in control, no matter how upset your child is. The key is to speak and act firmly and lovingly at the same time. For example, "I can understand you're upset that I discovered this, but we have to deal with what I found. I'm doing this because I love you and want you to be safe, and I'm not going to stand aside and let you continue."

CHAPTER 5

Causes of an Eating Disorder

Whose fault is it that your child has an eating disorder? What caused the eating disorder? Eating disorders are, in some ways, quite simple. While there may be a complex combination of factors that play a role, eating disorders are a brain disorder. There's a common saying that genes load the gun for an eating disorder while environment pulls the trigger. Genes and biology play a significant role in predisposing someone to an eating disorder.

Looking for an Answer

For years, the common refrain was that anorexia, or any other eating disorder for that matter, was always caused by an overbearing, overwrought mother who didn't have her own life to lead. That theory no longer holds water. Part of the reason there is no single, simple cure for eating disorders lies in the fact that there is no single, simple cause of eating disorders. In the last decade, dozens of theories about the potential causes of eating disorders have been debunked.

The Search for a Cure

In some cases, if you can identify what the cause of a problem is, you can correctly approach and perhaps even fix it. But as James Lock, MD, PhD, director of psychiatric services at the Comprehensive Eating Disorders Program at Lucile Packard Children's Hospital and an associate professor of child psychiatry, explains, "a lot of times we aren't able to know the cause of something and we still need to be able to go in and address it. For example, we don't know why this particular person developed this particular XYZ cancer, but we go in anyway and address. Lots of medical procedures are done without knowing the ultimate cause and by removing the problem. It would be great to know why and I would like to know why. In the meantime, as a practical guy, we have to work with the tools we have at hand."

The Evidence Reveals

Eating disorders are brain disorders whose exact mechanisms are not yet clear, much in the same way that bipolar disorder, autism, and depression are all known brain disorders with much left to discover. As one researcher explained, "We know about 2 percent of what there is to know about eating disorders. We know what it looks like. We are starting to learn how to treat it. And we know what doesn't cause it."

The Blame Game

Eating disorders have been recorded in human history for over a thousand years. In the Middle Ages, women who starved themselves were thought to be holy, while in the Victorian era, women with eating disorders were thought to be experiencing a mental state known as "hysteria." It hasn't been until the last few decades that research has clearly proven the cause is primarily biological.

Discarded Theories

There are almost as many theories for eating disorders as there have been researchers. Men who were vain, little girls who don't want to grow up because they are scared of their sexuality—you name it, it's been theorized as a cause for eating disorders. There is no evidence to suggest that eating disorders are a result of these commonly named bad guys:

- Overbearing mothers
- Absent fathers
- Early child abuse
- Sexual trauma
- Peer pressure
- Unspoken desire to remain childlike
- Unresolved internal conflict
- Fear of sexuality
- Thin models
- A need for control

Laying Blame

If your friend's daughter made it into Harvard University, you might well go to her for parenting advice. After all, she must have done something right to raise such a talented, bright, and well-rounded child. But as Laura Collins, the author of *Eating with Your Anorexic* and mother of an anorexic, explains, you probably won't ask the mother of an anorexic for parenting advice. Why not? Well, the assumption is that she probably did something wrong, if not to cause the eating disorder, then at least to exacerbate it.

Dear old Mom is the common villain when looking for a place to lay the blame for a child's eating disorder, and it has been for years. It's a common refrain, and the only problem with it is that it isn't true. It probably began when anxious mothers brought their children to doctors and mental health professionals, insisting that something was wrong. Since it often took multiple professionals months, if not years, to get a diagnosis, the providers often saw emotional, frustrated, and concerned parents whose children were actively dying in front of them. In comparison to the parents of "normal" children these practitioners may have frequently seen, the mothers looked overinvolved and too enmeshed in their child's lives. Of course, if they weren't, the children would have died already.

Did I cause my child's eating disorder?
No. Eating disorders are complex neurobiological disorders that, in many cases, have a genetic component. Other than as a giver of genetic material, parents are not to blame, and if a mental or physical health care provider insists otherwise, find a replacement.

If parents of a child with an eating disorder learn nothing else, it needs to be this: parents do not cause eating disorders.

Biology Rules

Eating disorders are inherited illnesses. However, trauma, personality traits, family dynamics, and societal influences, among other factors, can all play a role in the eating disorder's progression and in the child's recovery. The genetic link does not mean that there's no hope, but it does mean that eating disorders are very complex, and parents should be aware of this as they prepare to do battle.

Genetics
Many parents do not realize that genetics play a prominent role in increasing someone's vulnerability to an eating disorder. So while it's important to raise your kids in an environment that doesn't focus on appearance or dieting, eating disorders are first and fundamentally brain disorders.

 Fact

Researchers have found there is a higher risk for anorexia nervosa among men with a twin sister than among other men or even those with a twin brother.

Personality Traits

Was your child born with a propensity toward perfectionism, rigidity, or inflexibility about plan changes? Some people have personality traits and tendencies that may predispose themselves to disordered eating. While this may prove to be beneficial in academic settings where structure and determination are rewarded, those inborn traits, when combined with a brain wired for an eating disorder, may prove to be difficult.

At eleven, Juliet was teased for being chubby, and when she found a book on anorexia, she used it as a road map to how to become anorexic. Just a year later, she had lost twenty pounds and was religiously calorie counting. She sees that event as the trigger that started her eating disorder. However, a lot of children are overweight as a child and get teased at school but do not develop an eating disorder. While the teasing and subsequent dieting may have been the beginning, it is likely that she was already at risk for developing an eating disorder.

Researchers have identified a number of psychological factors that may contribute to eating disorders:

- Low self-esteem or feelings of inadequacy
- Feelings of a lack of control over life
- Depression, anger, anxiety, or loneliness
- A seemingly endless quest for perfection

If you have children who have perfectionist tendencies, are very rigid in their personal habits, or who can become obsessive, these factors may contribute to having difficulty eating in a healthy manner, and your child should be monitored more carefully.

Mental Illness

Children and teens with symptoms of anxiety, depression, and obsessive-compulsive disorder (OCD) often have disordered eating behaviors. It is not known why there is a link, only that there is. Parents whose children have an eating disorder should have their children evaluated for one of these concurrent conditions as well, and parents whose children have one of these mental health issues, or others, should see if disordered eating is manifested in their behaviors as well.

Messages Matter

Young people who are susceptible to eating disorders, whether through genetic predisposition, emotional regulation difficulties, family dynamics, or some combination of some or all these factors, are extremely vulnerable to the messages found in the media.

Ashley Solomon, PsyD, a therapist who specializes in the treatment of eating disorders, explains, "First, it's very important to understand that the media does not cause eating disorders. No direct causal link has been established connecting images of Victoria's Secret models to anorexia, or Internet diet ads to a rise in bulimia. This does not mean that the media doesn't have an important role in eating disorders via the way that we feel about our bodies. Some research does suggest a causal link between media images and body dissatisfaction. They have been primed through various mechanisms to identify thin as an ideal, and, too often, children and teenagers tend to overvalue it. Those with eating disorders take these messages to the extreme and are willing to put other things— and sometimes everything—on the line to achieve that ideal."

Peer Influence

Anne, whose bulimia started at fourteen, described her experience attending her local high school. "A week into high school and I had lost any scrap of self-esteem I had left. I was jealous of everyone. I compared myself to every single girl who walked by me. I turned my focus on trying to look good. If I wasn't pretty, popular, smart, funny, or vivacious like other girls my age, I yearned desperately to be pretty, to be like everyone else. That's when I started changing my food intake.

"People started to take notice. The other girls would see that I had healthy lunches and they would ask me for advice or guidance on how they should eat or how did I stay so thin. It made me feel good. This is my thing. This is what I am good at. I felt proud and successful and it drove me to become more rigid. I don't know when it changed from being healthy to anorexia. I didn't think about it really until I stopped getting my period."

Social Factors

There are a number of social factors that many mental health professionals feel may contribute to the development of eating disorders, including:

- Cultural pressures that glorify thinness and place significant value on obtaining the "perfect" body
- Narrow definitions of beauty that include only women and men of specific body weights and shapes
- Cultural norms that value people on the basis of physical appearance and not inner qualities and strengths

 Question

What would you sacrifice to be the "perfect" weight?
A recent study found that more than half of women surveyed in the United States would trade a year of their life in order to permanently lose twenty pounds.

Media Matters

Young girls are exposed to 400 to 600 media images per day, and a recent survey found only 2 percent of women in the world would describe themselves as "beautiful." The messages, explains Rosie Molinary, author of *Beautiful You: A Daily Guide to Radical Self-Acceptance*, are still really rooted in displaying thinness and even frailty, both emotionally and physically, in women. "The obsession of following celebrities has made us believe that every woman can and should lose her baby weight in just a week, that these bodies are attainable with just a little discipline, that perfect skin is just a cleanser away if we would just commit ourselves to the process."

More Than a Picture

At the very least, there is a strong correlation between viewing media images and feelings about one's body. Specifically, greater time spent in media consumption has been linked to greater feelings of body dissatisfaction. This is, of course, a complicated issue, as those who dislike their bodies may be more socially isolated and then spend more time watching television, for example, than going out with friends. Regardless, a link has consistently been demonstrated.

The mechanism by which media harms our positive feelings toward our bodies is unclear, but working with patients has suggested that there are various ways that the two intersect. When children are surrounded by images of "ideal beauty" being portrayed as emaciation or unnaturally muscular (for men), it is not surprising that feelings of body shame emerge. Our culture not only promotes an extremely unrealistic ideal of beauty, but it sees beauty as currency.

In nearly every form of media you can find examples of how beauty (equated as being thin) achieves positive results—the most positive results. Those who are considered beautiful are assigned various other traits, whether they deserve them or not. They are often considered more capable, more desirable, more honest, more sociable, and so on, and receive rewards for this—attention, career success, or money. You have to think not only about the fact that a young girl wants to look like a cover model but why she does. It's not just that the model is beautiful (though likely highly artificially enhanced), but it is also about what it means for her to be beautiful—what does that give her?

 Fact

Research is beginning to show that even indirect media exposure, such as having friends who watch a lot of TV, might be more damaging to a teenager's body image. Disordered eating isn't contagious through social networking, but it can be one more factor when a child is already vulnerable.

"I believe that the media has a responsibility to be mindful of their consumers," says Solomon. "So while the media cannot not cause eating disorders, it can work collaboratively to portray human beings with dignity and respect and facilitate a culture in which weight and shape are seen as only one of many aspects of a person."

What's in the Way of Recovery?

Across the world, there are researchers studying the causes of eating disorders and the paths to recovery. Parents' responsibilities are to their own children in terms of knowing and following evidence-based treatment. Ultimately, understanding the cause of a child's eating disorder is not as important as what steps are needed to initiate recovery.

"I wanted to know why," said Scott, whose daughter Kim had binge eating disorder. "I thought if I could see a schematic of her brain and see where the wires were crossed, then I could let go of the shame and guilt I was feeling. I had to realize that my focus needed to be not on what caused the eating disorder but what might get in the way of her healing. That was a big step for me, and for her, I think."

Personal History

Eating disorders often begin after a young person has experienced some sort of stressful event, even something that parents wouldn't necessarily see as traumatic, such as changing schools. Steve, whose son, Carl, developed an eating disorder in the fifth grade, could, in hindsight, see the beginning of what became a several-year battle with anorexia. "He went to an elementary school close to our house. He knew all the kids there. We knew all the parents. It was a great environment and he loved everything about it. When he started middle school, he went to another part of town. It was a good school, but it was a completely different set of kids. That's what started it. He was in a new place with new kids. He was like a lot of kids and was growing up and out and up and out. That was what started it."

These events, when they occur in a child predisposed to an eating disorder, may need to be addressed as a part of recovery:

- Troubled family and personal relationships
- Difficulty expressing emotions and feelings
- A history of being teased or ridiculed based on size, weight, or appearance
- A history of physical or sexual abuse
- A history of being praised based on size, weight, or appearance
- A single traumatic event
- A two- to three-year period of intense pain or stress
- An extended period of emotional pain
- The onset of a mood disorder

 Essential

There is evidence that gay, bisexual, and transgendered teens are at risk for depression, addictions, and eating disorders. The GLBT National Help Center provides help and resources for GLBT and questioning individuals through its youth talkline (1-800-246-PRIDE).

Family Dynamics

Family dynamics may no doubt play a role in eating disorders, often because there is a genetic link with eating disorders. A child may already have the genetic wiring and personality traits that will significantly predispose her to an eating disorder later in life. If you add in a mom or dad who is actively engaging in disordered eating behavior, or focusing an extreme amount of time and energy on weight and dieting, then the wheels are set spinning sooner in the child's life.

An Inability to Cope

A child with an eating disorder generally has no other tools in her emotional toolbox with which to deal with life stressors. Some children have more stressors than others or fewer tools than others due to a genetic blip, a traumatic event, or the misfortune of being seated next to the neighborhood bully on the bus for three years in a row. Whatever the reason, there is a part of every person who has an eating disorder who accepts disordered eating as a way of dealing with uncomfortable feelings. Lisa developed binge eating disorder at fifteen after failing several classes and remembers thinking, "I felt like a disappointment and a loser. I felt directionless and lonely and suddenly I couldn't stop eating. I found myself in stores buying things I hadn't eaten in years. I would just eat and eat and eat. I was eating my emotions. I was eating my sadness, and I was just drowning myself in food." Beyond nutrition, part of the recovery process is learning new ways of coping with fear, anger, and frustration.

Perhaps the best question to ask is not why a child has developed an eating disorder but what is getting in the way of the child getting better.

CHAPTER 6

Facing Reality

When a parent suspects that his or her child has an eating disorder, it can feel overwhelming. This is not the dream you had for your child. You may have suspected it for a while and have finally put the clues together, or it may be a complete shock to you. As tempting as it is to run for cover, denial is not an option. It's time to get to work. As your child's parent, you will encounter many health care providers, counselors, and eating disorder professionals along the way, but, ultimately, whether or not your child is diagnosed and treated appropriately falls on your shoulders.

Coming to the Truth

"I hate to admit it, but at first, I didn't think it was that big of a deal," explained Wendy, whose daughter had anorexia. "This sounds horrible, I know. But she did need to lose thirty pounds, and so many people complimented her on her weight loss. It was like that diet was the switch and then she just couldn't stop. I feel horrible for getting excited about her weight loss. Now she's lost another twenty pounds and I don't see any sign of her stopping."

While everyone has seen the handful of pictures of emaciated teenagers on tabloid television shows, those young sufferers are not a reflection of what most eating disorder sufferers look like. The problem with those heartbreaking but sensational portrayals is that they can lead to a false sense of security when your own children do not look nearly as sick as the ones on television. Many eating disorder sufferers don't necessarily even look as though they have an eating disorder. More importantly, your child doesn't have to be emaciated to be at a high risk for illness or death. Once a parent learns the signs and symptoms of an eating disorder, then the next step is to learn about the risks and how to find out if your child has one.

Long-Term Effects of Anorexia

Anorexia nervosa can be deadly. In anorexia nervosa, the mortality rate is roughly 10 percent, and patients are at an increased risk of death from cancer, endocrine causes, cardiovascular problems, respiratory problems, gastrointestinal issues, urogenital problems, autoimmune disorders, substance abuse, and suicide. Chronic or long-term anorexia nervosa reduces life expectancy by fifteen to twenty-five years.

Long-term effects include:

- Thinning of the bones (osteopenia or osteoporosis)
- Brittle hair and nails
- Dry and yellowish skin
- Growth of fine hair over body (lanugo)
- Mild anemia as well as muscle weakness and loss
- Severe anemia
- Low blood pressure; slowed breathing and pulse
- Drop in internal body temperature, causing a person to feel cold all the time
- Neurological problems
- Malnutrition
- Death

Heart disease is the most common cause of death in people with anorexia. In extreme cases of anemia, the bone marrow drastically reduces its production of new blood cells. It can cause a life-threatening condition called pancytopenia, an abnormal deficiency in red blood cells, white blood cells, and platelets.

 Essential

Anorexia nervosa causes potentially serious eye damage, and it isn't clear whether the eye damage shows initial stages of progressive blindness or if macular changes will improve once the eating disorder is resolved.

Long-Term Effects of Bulimia

"I started purging when I was thirteen years old. I was already dieting and then I read a *Seventeen* magazine about the 'dangers of bulimia' and all I saw was bulimia and its benefits. From that day forward I was bulimic. I would exercise until I passed out, eat any morsel of food I could find, and then purge. My mom knew about it and sent me to a counselor once, but we never talked about it. Not once. My eating disorder became my best friend, always by my side, and helped me look good, too. Now, fifteen years later, I can't stop. I can sit one day with my therapist, dietitian, best friend, anyone in the world and tell them I'll never do it again, and I mean it. I can look at myself in the mirror and promise I'll never do it again. I pray to God and promise Him I'll never harm my body that way again. And then I do. It's horrible and dangerous and I wish mine would have been treated a long time ago. I think it's too late for me now," admits Susan.

According to the National Institute of Mental Health, health problems that may develop over time in people with bulimia include:

- Chronically inflamed and sore throat
- Swollen glands in the neck and below the jaw
- Worn tooth enamel and increasingly sensitive and decaying teeth as a result of exposure to stomach acids

- Ulcers and gastroesophageal reflux disorder
- Intestinal distress and irritation from laxative abuse
- Kidney problems from diuretic abuse
- Severe dehydration from purging of fluids
- Malnutrition
- Stomach rupture
- Mallory-Weiss syndrome: bleeding where the esophagus connects to the stomach due to tears in the mucous membrane from violent or prolonged retching or vomiting. It is often painless and can be fatal.
- Death

In bulimia nervosa, the mortality rate is much higher than reported because many times death by stomach rupture, acute gastric dilation, and pancreatitis are not reported as being related to bulimia.

 Fact

Eighty percent of people with bulimia nervosa report one or more severe GI complaints, including delayed gastric emptying, constipation, elevated liver enzymes, acute pancreatitis, complications from vomiting, gastric rupture, Mallory-Weiss tears, esophageal and or gastric bleeding, increased amylase (liver enzymes), parotid swelling, and erosion of dental enamel.

Long-Term Effects of BED

Binge eating disorder can lead to a wide variety of social, emotional, and physical problems. People who have binge eating disorder are more likely to report health issues, stress, insomnia, and suicidal ideation than are people who do not have an eating disorder. Depression, anxiety, and substance abuse are also common.

Long-term effects of binge eating disorder include:

- Weight gain, which can lead to obesity
- Diabetes
- Osteoarthritis
- Gallbladder problems
- Heart disease
- Certain types of cancer
- Hypertension
- High cholesterol levels
- Malnutrition
- Osteoarthritis
- Joint and muscle pain
- Death

 Essential

It is critical to understand that binge eating disorder is dangerous but in a different way than with anorexia nervosa and bulimia nervosa. The latter two may place your child at a more immediate risk for health problems, while many of the risks from binge eating disorder are related to obesity.

A Fatal Disorder

What many parents do not realize is that an eating disorder can kill their child. In fact, 10 percent of those with an eating disorder will die from it. The longer a person has an eating disorder, the higher the chances that he or she will die from it. Eating disorders, especially anorexia nervosa, increase a person's risk for suicide. Studies have shown that women with anorexia are more likely to have suicidal thoughts than those with bulimia or other disorders. What's worse is that when people with an eating disorder attempt suicide, they are likely to attempt using more extreme measures in an effort to ensure their success.

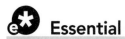 **Essential**

F.E.A.S.T. (Families Empowered and Supporting Treatment for Eating Disorders) is an excellent resource for parents who wish to educate themselves about eating disorders and evidence-based treatment. Check out their website at *www.feast-ed.org*.

Next Step: Talk to Your Child

Unfortunately, getting from suspecting that your child has an eating disorder to having a diagnosis in hand can be exhausting. Only after having a conversation with your child, seeing a physician, and getting a diagnosis can you and your family begin the work of recovery. Getting a diagnosis is necessary, not only to start treatment for the disorder, but especially if you want health insurance to pay for any part of treatment.

If you suspect that your son or daughter has an eating disorder, then you need to have that conversation with your child. It is important to begin an open dialogue about what you perceive to be as a potential problem. While your emotions may be sky-high, you need to wait until you can have a noncombative conversation that isn't clouded by extreme emotions on your part. You can feel scared and overwhelmed, but confronting your child when you are in the midst of feeling overwhelmed by those emotions isn't likely to benefit anyone or solicit an honest response.

Have the Talk

There is no perfect template for how to ask your child if he or she might have an eating disorder. There are, however, some guidelines. First, don't use the term "eating disorder." Your child may not recognize her behavior as fitting into those guidelines and may be more likely to deny there is a problem. Instead, ask your child if he is having a problem with food. Talk about the signs you see and express why you are concerned. For example: "I notice that you're not eating dinner with our family anymore. What's going on?"

She Says She's Fine

One of the many problems with an eating disorder is that it isn't just a physical problem; it is also a mental health issue. Therefore, expect that if you ask a child with an eating disorder if there is a problem with her eating, she may not actually feel as though there is a problem, even if she is starving herself, binging, or purging. Some children with an eating disorder have even personalized their eating disorder and refer to it as a friend or companion.

"I had done a great job of hiding Ana (a reference to anorexia)," explains Claire. "I wore baggy clothes, I came home from school late and said I ate at a friend's house, and I even talked about what I had for lunch at school. When she confronted me, I panicked. I wasn't going to tell her the truth. I didn't want her to take Ana away from me. I could tell she wasn't sure, but it bought me another two months until she really freaked out."

 Essential

Closely monitor any changes in your child's or teen's eating habits. Be on the lookout for seemingly "positive" changes including becoming a vegetarian, skipping dessert, or reducing fat intake. Those can all be signs of an emerging eating disorder.

If you expect your child to fling open his arms in gratitude, thank you for your questions, reveal the full extent of his disorder, and immediately agree to counseling, you will probably be disappointed. Instead, even in the midst of denial or even anger, you must let your child know that you hear what she is saying, that you love and support her, but that you may need to call in some other people to help you know what is going on and what to do about it. The bottom line is this: if your child's attitude or behavior regarding food is causing harm or has the potential to cause harm, then your child needs help.

In Search of a Diagnosis

If you believe your child is in the beginning stages of an eating disorder, the temptation is to wait until he earns a "real" diagnosis. If left untreated or improperly treated, the disordered eating can become a life-threatening illness. Begin treatment at the time you believe is necessary so that your child achieves complete, lasting recovery treatment. Remember to trust your parental instincts.

The diagnosis of an eating disorder is difficult for the child and the family. No parent wants to hear that his or her child has an eating disorder; however, getting a diagnosis has a positive side: Now you know. Diagnosis is the first step in getting treatment for your child. First of all, the eating problem may not even be an eating disorder at all. If your child is quickly losing weight and isn't limiting intake or purging, there could be a medical problem that needs investigating.

Start with Your Physician

For most parents, the first place to begin is with the child's primary care physician. Call your physician's office and ask if your physician has experience diagnosing and treating eating disorders. A pediatrician who works with a number of adolescents may well be experienced, but so may a family physician. The best thing to do is to call and ask before you make an appointment.

 Essential

If you ask your physician for a referral to a physician who specializes in adolescents, ask your health care provider for help in getting an emergency appointment, as well as in getting copies of your child's medical records.

Physician Limitations

It is not always realistic to trust your child's pediatrician to spot an eating disorder because most physicians or even pediatricians do not have specialized training in eating disorders. As such, they are unlikely to be able to identify an eating disorder until it is in its advanced stages. They are more likely to be able to diagnose one once it has been brought to their attention, but physicians will still overlook classic eating disorder signs and symptoms such as weight loss, missed menstrual periods, or failure to grow. Consider taking your child to a pediatrician or adolescent medicine physician who specializes in eating disorders.

The Medical History Interview

The first step in making a diagnosis of an eating disorder is the medical interview of the patient and the family. The physician will ask a series of questions about whether the child has typical symptoms of an eating disorder. The doctor will try to assess the severity of the symptoms, how long they have been present, and whether they are getting worse. The physician may ask you how the symptoms have affected your child's overall health. For example, a child may have had weight loss, low energy levels and fatigue, or the absence of a menstrual cycle.

The physician will also likely take a social history, such as where and with whom the child lives, school attendance, substance abuse, or any additional stressors in the home. This will not be the last time that your family's business becomes public, and it can be difficult to be honest. Remember, no family is perfect, and your physician is not going to judge you or your parenting but is simply trying to gather as much information as possible. The ultimate goal is to get the right help for your child, and this is where you begin.

Fact

Teenagers with an eating disorder are more likely to have substance abuse problems. For example, those who were anorexic were 1.6 times more likely to have problems with alcohol, but bulimics were 3.1 times as likely. A substance abuse screening is an important part of an initial assessment for your teen.

Expect Dishonesty

It is highly likely that your child will not be honest with the physician. Eating disorders are a neurobiological disorder; add malnutrition to the mix and expect cognitive dysfunction. Whether your child is not eating, binge eating and then purging, or just binge eating, he is not likely to either admit the behavior or willingly accept the need for help. This can be a problem as the physician may believe what the child says and view you as being overprotective or even overbearing.

Physical Examination

The next step in your child's evaluation is a complete physical examination. This usually includes:

- Height and weight check
- Reflex tests
- Listening to the heart for slow heart rate or abnormal heart rhythms
- Looking at the fingernails for a bluish tint (indicating low oxygen)
- Checking for dry skin (may indicate dehydration) or growth of lanugo (downy hair) over body
- Looking inside the mouth to see whether teeth have any erosion from possible purging
- Blood pressure reading

Understanding Lab Tests

Laboratory tests are generally performed in order to get a more accurate indicator of how an eating disorder may have affected your child's overall health. Typical lab tests include blood and urine tests, although additional tests, such as electrocardiograms or bone scans, may need to be performed.

Blood Tests

Your doctor's office may do a blood draw, or the physician may send you to a freestanding lab or hospital lab to draw blood. Several vials will be drawn and a number of tests will be run. The most likely tests series that will be run is the CBC, which measures the size, shape, and number of different types of cells (red blood cells, white blood cells, platelets) in the blood. The different types of white blood cells (such as neutrophils, lymphocytes) may also be measured. Plus, a CBC test provides other information about the blood, including the amount of hematocrit (the volume of blood that is made up of red blood cells) and the amount of hemoglobin (the protein that carries oxygen in the blood) in the blood. Low hemoglobin levels indicate anemia, which can be serious and is common in those with eating disorders.

Another panel of blood tests that are often run include a basic metabolic panel (BMP), which is a set of eight tests. The basic metabolic panel (BMP) checks blood urea nitrogen (BUN) and creatinine, or waste products the kidneys filter out of the blood. If there are increased concentrations of creatinine in the blood, there may be a decrease in kidney function.

A BMP also measures electrolyte levels. Electrolytes are essential minerals that can become depleted with dehydration and starvation. Electrolytes, particularly calcium and potassium, are critical for regulating heart rhythm, muscle contraction, and brain function. Abnormal electrolyte levels also may occur with heart disease, kidney disease, or dehydration.

Electrolyte levels tested usually include:

- Potassium
- Calcium
- Sodium
- Phosphorus
- Magnesium

Other tests may include a thyroid function test that can check for an overactive thyroid gland (hyperthyroid), which may mean that your child has a problem gaining weight, or an underactive thyroid (hypothyroid), which may indicate a problem losing weight. Blood sugar levels or cholesterol may also be tested.

Urine Tests

A urinalysis is usually performed in the doctor's office, but like the blood tests, it can be performed in a lab. A urinalysis can identify a variety of urinary tract disorders or systemic diseases. It can also determine kidney function, urine sugar, and ketone levels.

Ketone levels are important because ketones can accumulate in the blood when the body is deprived of food and nutrients. The presence of ketones indicates that the body is using its own fat for energy and can lead to ketoacidosis, which can be dangerous.

Bone Density Scan

What many people do not realize is that eating disorders can do a significant amount of damage to bones. Almost all (90 percent) women with anorexia will experience osteopenia, or loss of bone minerals, and 40 percent currently have osteoporosis, which is a more serious and advanced loss of bone density, making them more prone to fractures and more susceptible to infections. The damage is long term as well since up to two-thirds of children and adolescent boys and girls with anorexia will have stunted growth and/or fail to develop strong bones during their critical growing period. In general, the less the patient weighs, the more severe the bone loss will be. People who purge face even higher risks for bone loss. When eating disorders cause amenorrhea, or no menstrual cycle, the chances of developing osteoporosis at an early age are increased.

 Fact

A bone density scan, also called a DXA (dual-energy X-ray absorptiometry), is way of measuring bone density loss and can identify osteoporosis, or abnormal loss of bony tissue resulting in fragile, porous bone.

Electrocardiogram or Echocardiogram

Your child's physician may want to perform an electrocardiogram or echocardiogram, which will need to be done at a hospital or at a cardiologist's office. An EKG checks for heartbeat irregularities, especially if there is any suspicion of shortness of breath, palpitations, or any pressure or pain in the chest.

A Psychiatric Evaluation

A psychiatrist, psychologist, or counselor may be the next step in diagnosing your child's eating disorder. Your health insurance may determine which type of professional you use. An evaluation is made based on behaviors that are presented in relationship to physical, genetic, environmental, social, cognitive (thinking), emotional, and educational components that may be affected.

 Alert

You must see a mental health professional who has experience diagnosing eating disorders, or the visit will be a waste of resources. For an eating disorder specialist near you, go to Ed Referral at *www .edreferral.com*.

The evaluation may include:

- Description of behaviors present (that is, when do the behaviors occur, how long do the behaviors last, what are the conditions in which the behaviors most often occur)
- Description of symptoms noted (physical and psychiatric symptoms)
- Discussion of effects of behaviors/symptoms as related to the following: school performance, relationships and interactions with others (parents, siblings, classmates, teachers), and activities
- Psychiatric interview
- Personal and family history of emotional, behavioral, or developmental disorders
- Complete medical history, including description of the child's overall physical health, list of any other illnesses or conditions present, and any treatments currently being administered

The Diagnostic Criteria

Physicians and psychologists are expected to make a diagnosis based on a certain set of criteria that have been established in the *Diagnostic and Statistical Manual of Mental Disorders* (DSM-IV), a manual published by the American Psychiatric Association (APA) that includes all currently recognized mental health disorders. This matters to you because the coding system utilized by the DSM-IV corresponds with codes from the *International Classification of Diseases*, commonly referred to as the ICD, the coding used for health insurance purposes. In other words, the diagnosis affects insurance reimbursement. The DSM-IV lists very specific guidelines for the diagnosis of anorexia, bulimia, and EDNOS (eating disorder not otherwise specified).

DSM-IV Criteria for Anorexia Nervosa (307.1)

The diagnostic criteria for anorexia focuses heavily on determining which signs and symptoms are present in the patient. Some attention is paid to the patient's perception and attitudes, but it is less critical than the actual disordered eating behavior and results.

- Refuse to maintain body weight at or above a minimally normal weight for age and height
- Intense fear of gaining weight or becoming fat, even though underweight
- Disturbance in the way in which one's body weight/shape is experienced
- Postmenarchal females, amenorrhea (the absence of three consecutive menstrual cycles)

TYPE
- *Restricting Type*: During the current episode of Anorexia Nervosa, the person has not regularly engaged in binge eating or purging behavior (self-induced vomiting or misuse of laxatives, diuretics, or enemas).
- *Binge Eating/Purging Type*: During the current episode of Anorexia Nervosa, the person has regularly engaged in binge eating or purging behavior.

DSM IV Criteria for Bulimia Nervosa (307.51)

Bulimia nervosa is diagnosed slightly differently than anorexia nervosa, primarily because weight loss does not typically accompany bulimia. Instead, a diagnosis is usually made after taking a health history, analyzing the patient's binging and purging behaviors, and considering their beliefs and attitudes.

- Recurrent episodes of binge eating characterized by both of the following:

- Eating, in a discrete period of time (e.g. within any two-hour period), an amount of food that is larger than most people would eat during a similar period of time
  - A sense of lack of control over eating during the episode

- Recurrent inappropriate compensatory behaviors
- The binge and inappropriate compensatory behaviors both occur, on average, at least twice a week for three months

TYPE

- *Purging Type*: The person has regularly engaged in self-induced vomiting or the misuse of laxatives, diuretics, or enemas.
- *Nonpurging Type*: The person has used other inappropriate compensatory behavior but has not regularly engaged in self-induced vomiting or misused laxatives, diuretics, or enemas.

Eating Disorder Not Otherwise Specified (307.50)

This diagnosis includes disorders of eating that do not meet the criteria for the above two eating disorder diagnoses. Examples include:

- For female patients, all of the criteria for anorexia nervosa are met except that the patient has regular menses.
- All of the criteria for anorexia nervosa are met except that, despite significant weight loss, the patient's current weight is in the normal range.
- All of the criteria for bulimia nervosa are met except that the binge eating and inappropriate compensatory mechanisms occur less than twice a week or for less than three months.
- The patient has normal body weight and regularly uses inappropriate compensatory behavior after eating small amounts of food (such as self-induced vomiting after consuming two cookies).

- The patient engages in repeatedly chewing and spitting out, but not swallowing, large amounts of food.

Binge Eating Disorder

Listed in the DSM-IV appendix as a diagnosis for further study, binge eating disorder is defined as uncontrolled binge eating without emesis or laxative abuse. It is often, but not always, associated with obesity symptoms. A proposed diagnostic criteria for binge eating disorder is currently being used by some practitioners and includes:

RECURRENT EPISODES OF BINGE EATING CHARACTERIZED BY BOTH:
- Eating, in a discrete period of time (e.g., <two hours), an amount of food that is definitely larger than most people would eat under similar circumstances
- A sense of lack of control over eating during the episode

These episodes are associated with three (or more) of the following:

- Eating much more rapidly than normal
- Eating until feeling uncomfortably full
- Eating large amounts of food when not feeling physically hungry
- Eating alone because of being embarrassed by how much one is eating
- Marked distress regarding binge eating

The binge eating occurs, on average, at least one time a week for three months. And it is not associated with the recurrent use of inappropriate compensatory behavior and does not occur exclusively during the course of either anorexia nervosa or bulimia nervosa.

Does She or Doesn't She?

One of the things that may happen when you intervene at the first sign of your child's eating disorder is that your child may not meet the full criteria for anorexia nervosa, bulimia nervosa, or binge eating disorder. Instead, she may be diagnosed with eating disorder not otherwise specified (EDNOS), or she may not be diagnosed with an eating disorder at all. This does not mean that your child does not have an eating disorder, that the disordered eating isn't serious, or that immediate, aggressive intervention isn't necessary.

What No Diagnosis Means

It may mean that your child is in the beginning stages of the eating disorder and does not yet meet the criteria, or it may mean that the physician does not have enough experience with diagnosing eating disorders. Fortunately, it is generally not difficult to get a diagnosis for eating disorder not otherwise specified (EDNOS), which may appease your health insurance company.

 Essential

A full 50 percent of children who have disordered eating habits that affect their health do not meet the diagnostic criteria for an eating disorder.

Now What?

"If I had one piece of advice I could give to another mother whose child is diagnosed with an eating disorder, it is first to just breathe. You are strong and loving and loved and have all of the resources you need to care for your child, even if you don't know what they are right now," offers Stephanie, whose son has bulimia.

Once it has been confirmed that your child has an eating disorder, then treatment must begin.

CHAPTER 7

Steps Toward Treatment

"No man is an island," John Donne once said, and he was right—especially when it comes to parenting a child with an eating disorder. Regardless of a parent's education, occupation, intentions, or commitment, no parent—or set of parents—has all the resources, at least initially, to effectively diagnose, treat, and care for a child with an eating disorder. As parents, you are, however, in charge of your child's treatment and who you invite to be a part of your treatment team.

A New Attitude

When an eating disorder disrupts a family, it takes over. It is not a neat little illness that will quietly sit in the corner and mind its own business. Instead, it will affect and infect anyone in its way. While that may sound dramatic, many parents report that treating an eating disorder is the true-to-life equivalent of dragon slaying. "I've never been to war," says Christina, whose daughter Summer has binge eating disorder, "but I feel like I have. I did battle with an eating disorder. I had to tell myself a dozen times a day, 'This is not my daughter speaking, it's the eating disorder.' I knew if I gave an inch, the eating disorder would get stronger." Separating the eating disorder from the child is an important process when beginning treatment.

Prepare for Battle

When your child has an eating disorder, prepare yourself for the fact that there is nothing you can say that is going to fundamentally alter your child's thinking. Arguing, explaining, crying, and yelling, while all tempting, are not going to fix your child.

"I have a houseful of food and my child was in the next room starving to death. How could this happen? How can that happen in the twenty-first century? How could I let it happen," asked Tom, whose twelve-year-old son developed anorexia. "He was cold all the time. His fingers were cold, his lips were blue, and I was terrified I was going to have to watch him die. What was worse was that for the first time in his life, I couldn't help him."

Parents often can't help their children in the ways they may have been able to do so in the past. Pep talks, lectures, tears, and guilt trips may well have worked in the past, but these are no longer effective as parenting techniques. But that doesn't mean you can't be a good parent, it just means that there is absolutely nothing that you can say that will magically cure your child's disordered eating.

Tame the Anger

Terry Moore, who teaches cognitive behavioral therapy at Non-Violent Alternatives, Inc., in Indianapolis, teaches that all anger is a form of fear. Think about it. When you're running late for work and the driver in front of you insists on driving oh-so-slowly, that fear of getting in trouble at work becomes directed toward the driver and you start tailgating, honking your horn, and slamming your hands on the steering wheel. When your children's behavior scares you, the fear can quickly turn into frustration and even anger, especially after the third or fourth time you find laxatives and diet pills hidden in her room or another stash of cupcakes and other food hidden under the bed.

"I was in nursing school at the time my daughter's disordered eating began. Plus she was cutting herself," remembers Jane, whose daughter has been in recovery for over a year. "I was so angry and frustrated with her that I told her all of the months and thousands of dollars I had already spent in school were a waste since I was going to have to quit school to deal with her problems. Not surprisingly, it didn't work. Because my daughter loved me, I was sure that the guilt would be enough to wake her up. All that it did was make her feel worse." Be prepared to battle your own demons as you confront the eating disorder.

Early Intervention

The moment that you suspect your child has an eating disorder is the moment you have to act. It may be helpful to compare the eating disorder with another serious illness. If your child came to you saying she had found a suspicious lump somewhere on her body, your response would be to intervene immediately, aggressively, and with the most effective treatment possible. You would get diagnostic tests to confirm a diagnosis, find an oncologist, and research the most up-to-date and effective treatment regimen available. You wouldn't wait to see if the lump went away on its own, nor would you demand that the child stop having the lump. You could try, but it would be ineffectual and a waste of precious time.

As one father explains, "My advice to any family who suspects that their son or daughter has an eating disorder is to act. Act as quickly as you possibly can. One out of every ten people with an eating disorder will die from it. So many more people struggle and struggle mightily with it for probably the rest of their lives. It's the kind of thing that won't stop. The longer you wait to act, the harder it's going to be to overcome."

Immediate Action
Going back to the previous cancer analogy, the longer a person waits to receive treatment for cancer, the poorer the prognosis. The same is true for eating disorder treatment. The longer an eating dis-

order is left untreated, the more malnourished the child becomes, and the greater the likelihood of long-term effects, including osteoporosis, hypertension, heart problems, and more. Beyond the health problems, delay in receiving eating disorder treatment often means that the eating disorder becomes more entrenched and is more difficult to eradicate.

Aggressive Treatment

Evidence-based treatment must begin when a child has disordered eating. Effective treatment must be aggressive; that is, the parents cannot make a halfhearted commitment to treatment. Appropriate medical care, counseling, and nutrition are all key criteria for intervention. One particular treatment modality, family-centered therapy, is particularly aggressive and adopts a zero-tolerance policy toward any level of malnutrition. There is simply no possibility for a child to diet, skip meals, or cut out entire food groups. Aggressive treatment is grounded on the ideas that supervised and supported full nutrition is the best defense against an eating disorder, that nutrition is medicine, and that children and teenagers need to eat three substantial, nutritious, well-balanced meals every day in order to regain their health and well-being.

Effective Intervention

It may sound obvious, but for treatment to be effective, it must be based on research and evidence. Pleading with children and teens to eat, making deals with children, and engaging in negotiations with them regarding food is ineffective. More importantly, wasting time on ineffective approaches means that the child is sick for longer. Ineffective interventions spend days and weeks focusing on family dynamics, the root causes of the disorder, and exploration of potential triggers while ignoring that a child is not eating. An appropriate intervention acknowledges that the primary concern is making sure your child is well-nourished and physically healthy.

Learning to Listen

Carolyn Costin, MA, encourages parents to be honest when talking to their children about eating disorders. "It's okay to say 'I don't get it. But I am open and willing for you to help me understand.' We, looking from the outside, can see all of the things this eating disorder is doing to them. It's ruining their lives. It's taking so much away from them. It's almost like an alien has come in and turned them into a creature you don't know, and it's very hard to see what draws this child to an eating disorder. But as parents, we have to befriend the enemy, in a sense, so that we can understand this other part of our child. Think of it like this: keep your friends close and your enemies closer."

Begin the Battle

Battling with an eating disorder is more than a full-time job, and absolutely no one can go it alone. Therapist Ashley Solomon, PsyD, suggests thinking of this disease as a battle, just as one would describe battling cancer or other illnesses. This metaphor for working together to treat the eating disorder makes clear that parents need support. A one-man army is not going to be able to stand up to an illness that can ravage a child's mind and body. Parents need to enlist support on various fronts, and that will typically include, at minimum, a physician, mental health professional, and nutritionist.

 Fact

Before you can move forward with choosing a treatment approach and creating a treatment plan, making sure your child is medically stable is the first priority. A thorough physical examination must be performed, including height/weight checks, blood pressure reading, listening to heart and lung sounds, and lab work as indicated.

Treatment Options

As you look into treatment you will discover there are a number of treatment options available, including:

- Inpatient treatment
- Individual or group therapy
- Family therapy
- Eating disorder education
- Nutritional counseling
- Medical monitoring

Treatment Plans

You may hear the terms "treatment plan," or "individualized treatment plan" as you begin your research process. In general, a treatment plan is a medical and clinical plan usually designed by a team of physicians and clinicians, complete with goals and objectives focused on the patient achieving and maintaining long-term health and wellness. An individual treatment plan is specifically created for a particular patient and is continually assessed throughout the treatment process. As the parent, you bear ultimate responsibility for creating and upholding your child's eating disorder treatment plan, which may include:

- Thorough initial psychiatric evaluation
- Thorough initial physical examination
- Complete review of the patient's medical history
- Psychotherapeutic interventions for the individual and family
- Nutritional assessment and ongoing therapy
- Cognitive and dialectical behavior therapies
- Symptom management skills
- Ongoing psychiatric assessment, including medications as appropriate
- Creative arts, vocational therapy, and body image work

- Social skills and interpersonal relationship training
- Relapse prevention
- Close coordination of care and discharge planning with community-based treatment team

Choosing a Treatment Approach

Eating disorder treatment theories have continued to evolve over the last several decades, which means that some practitioners will not be up to date on the most effective eating disorder treatments. How is a parent to know what to do? Do you put your child in a residential treatment facility or commit him to a psychiatric facility? Are there other options? In the face of difficult questions, parents need to do what they would do if their child had any other potentially fatal medical problem: find the most effective treatment based on available research. This may, of course, be limited by time, travel ability, and financial resources.

Evidence-Based Practice

A common way to refer to such treatment is evidence-based practice. Evidence-based treatment methodologies will result in the most positive outcomes with the least cost in terms of suffering, time, and money. Generally, but not always, most of the professionals in a given field agree on the methodology as an accepted practice. That can be difficult when a condition like an eating disorder requires both medical and mental health intervention. Many therapists, even ones who received special training in eating disorders just a decade ago, are not up to date on either the latest research or most effective treatments. Too many families end up taking their child to multiple eating disorders specialists over a period of several months or even years. Try to avoid that exhausting waste of time and money by choosing your first care providers carefully.

Parents must understand possible treatment options to select the best option for their child.

Ask Questions

When confronted with a health problem for their child, parents typically turn to either their pediatrician, other parents, or even local community resources like a school guidance counselor or nurse. Eating disorders make that process trickier. In this situation, you cannot afford to have just anyone treat your child and risk doing more harm than good. It is appropriate to ask for referrals and suggestions from local resources, but know you will have to do your own vetting to make sure the providers meet your strict criteria. As you begin to collect information for local resources, start asking questions. Some sample questions include:

- What is the program's philosophy?
- What do they believe about eating disorders?
- What do they say about the causes of eating disorders?
- How do they treat eating disorders?
- What kinds of services do they offer after you've been through the program?
- What do they mean by "overweight" or "compulsive"?
- Does the program support dieting?

Warning Signs

F.E.A.S.T. (Families Empowered and Supporting Treatment of Eating Disorders) makes some recommendations for parents choosing treatment providers. Parents need to be intentional in choosing treatment providers who provide evidence-based practice and as such should not participate in any of these behaviors:

- Blame parents for causing eating disorders, either in part or as primary causal factor.
- Attribute disordered eating to dysfunctional family dynamics.
- List parents with inappropriate boundaries, parents with poor body image, enmeshed mothers, or distant fathers as causal factors.

- Use words that mean "cause" in place of "contribute to," "enable," "trigger," or "risk factor."
- Advise parents to leave treatment decisions like nutritional and weight decisions to children or to professionals.
- Advise parents not to be involved with food decisions.
- Advise parents that their children have to "want" to get better.
- Treat parents or their responsibilities differently than they would if their child had any other serious illness.

Finding a Dietitian

Parents get the best outcome when a multidisciplinary team including a physician, therapist, registered dietitian (RD), and psychiatrist, if needed, are working together to restore the physical and mental health of their child. Refeeding alone is not enough to fully cure the eating disorder. Many children and teens have had disordered thoughts about food and weight a year or so before the eating disorder symptoms begin, so their distorted thoughts about nutrition and physiology are firmly entrenched. The RD is the primary person on the team who can provide helpful resources regarding food, weight, activity and metabolism.

A registered dietitian can be extremely helpful to parents when they are refeeding a child with an eating disorder. The physician and therapist have typically had very limited training in nutrition or the refeeding process. Since nutrition is the initial focus of the child's treatment plan, it makes sense to have a nutrition expert involved. The RD will educate the parents about the physical effects of starvation and how different foods affect the gut, and she will work with them along the way to make the refeeding process easier and more tolerable for the child.

Treatment Role

After the initial evaluation, the RD communicates his or her nutrition and clinical assessment findings to the other team members and parents to aid in the diagnostic process. An RD who specializes in eating disorders is familiar with the DSM-IV criteria and will ask appropriate questions during the intake process. During treatment, the RD can develop a nutrition plan with the parent's input and will serve as the parent's coach and advocate during the refeeding process.

Once the child's weight is restored, the RD will begin to work with the child individually, using cognitive behavioral therapy to correct the child's distorted thoughts about food, weight, and exercise. She will also teach the client to be comfortable eating all foods in all types of social situations (such as pizza and cake at a party). Lastly, the RD will often do body image work to help the client accept and be comfortable with his healthy weight range. During the recovery phase, the RD will see the client periodically to monitor for signs of relapse and to provide support. She will help the client problem-solve new situations that arise involving food, such as eating in restaurants or eating in a college dorm.

Find a Nutritionist

It is imperative to find an RD who specializes in treating eating disorders, as these clinicians have had additional training in psychology that other RDs have not. It is ideal to find an RD who has worked at an eating disorders residential or inpatient facility, but if this is not possible, inquire as to the type and amount of training the RD has received in eating disorders. Usually the physician or therapist will be able to recommend an appropriate RD.

If you need help locating a nutritionist who specializes in eating disorders, try one of these online resources: *www.bulimia.com*, *www.aedweb.org*, *www.scandpg.org*, or *www.edreferral.com*.

CHAPTER 8

Finding Your Voice

If you've ever felt helpless when dealing with the health care industry, you aren't the only one. All patients who must learn to cope with any long-term illness need someone to promote, advocate for, and protect their health, safety, and patient rights. As a parent, you have a unique opportunity and obligation to advocate for your child.

Become an Advocate for Your Child

To become an advocate means to speak out about a need that someone has. As a parent of a child with an eating disorder, becoming an advocate means to speak out about your child's need, whether small or large, in an attempt to get assistance in meeting that need. Other people can become advocates as well, including grandparents, siblings, or other close friends or family members. Traditionally, however, parents are best able to serve as their child's advocate. When a child has a long-term health-related problem, families must learn to hone their advocacy skills to improve their child's quality of life.

A New Way of Thinking

Parenting a child with an eating disorder will likely force parents to act in roles they never before imagined. If you have never had many dealings with the medical community for example, you might be more likely to believe that you are obligated to do anything and everything that a health care professional suggests. Once you have been involved with the health care system for any period of any time, then you will learn that there are times the medical professionals, as well meaning as they are, will recommend treatment that is not evidence based, not appropriate for treating eating disorders, or not right for your child. It is your responsibility as your child's advocate to make the decision that is right for your family. Advocating for your child does not mean being a bully, nor does it mean an adversarial relationship has to be created. It does mean, however, that you retain the responsibility for your child's care.

Many parents may at least initially resist the idea of becoming their child's advocate. "I don't even have a college degree, much less a medical degree," says Sam, whose daughter has bulimia. "I will be the first one to say that I don't have the knowledge that a lot of doctors do, but what I do have is something no other doctor on the planet has. I know my daughter. I know when she's lying. I know when she feels overwhelmed and how she withdraws. Her mother and I are in this for the long haul. Nobody else can say that. Plus, we love her."

Why Advocate?

You, as a parent, do not need to have a medical degree or a counseling license to help your child. However, you do need to have a broad understanding of your child and your child's needs. Just what you need to advocate for will depend on your child's unique needs, your health care providers and their suggestions, and your health insurance policy requirements. It does require that you begin with the assumption that you are an equal partner in the decision-making process, and you have final say.

Do Your Homework

The first step in being an advocate for your child is to learn everything possible when you need to know it. While you do not need to become an expert on all things related to eating disorders, you do need to become an expert on your child and your child's eating disorder. Learning about an issue, whether that involves health insurance benefits, choosing a treatment resource, or navigating school concerns, will require you to learn exactly what you and your child's rights are. Becoming an advocate also means that you have to learn what to do and where to go if you need help asserting those rights. Once you become familiar with those rights, then the next step is to learn to communicate your perspective and decisions to the health care provider, health insurance companies, and others involved in your child's care.

Do Your Research

Visit reliable, evidence-based websites to research information related to eating disorder treatment. This is one place where Google probably isn't going to help you. While Google Scholar has a search option that lets you locate medical research studies on the topics that interest you, PubMed (*www.ncbi.nlm.nih.gov/pubmed*) is an easier online reference tool to use. PubMed, from the U.S. National Library of Medicine of the National Institutes of Health, allows you to type in your search terms and be given an extensive list of reliable research articles on the condition.

By clicking on a link to a research article, you will then be directed to the article's abstract, a paragraph-long article summary. At the bottom of each PubMed abstract is the "LinkOut" option. By clicking on "LinkOut," you are directed to where you can access the full text of the article. Many of the articles can be read free of charge, though some cannot be downloaded. Even if the free article is not accessible, the abstract will offer some information, and it may provide more questions for your next conversation with your child's health care provider.

Fact

Both Google and Yahoo! offer free news alerts that make it easy to keep up with the latest eating disorder treatments, research, and more, all delivered straight to your e-mail inbox.

Provider Research

Your primary health care provider may refer you to a counselor, eating disorder specialist, or therapist. An important part of advocating is making sure the professionals you bring into your family's life have the right to be there.

 Question

How do I get started finding information on physicians?
DocFinder (*www.docboard.org*) is a free online database that compiles information from more than twenty states, and it provides links to databases from other states. Most of the entries contain the following information about a physician: the doctor's specialty, address of the doctor's practice, school from which the doctor graduated, and the status of the doctor's license.

Take the time to review the clinicians' experiences, licenses, work history, and legal issues. Confirm that your child's clinicians are state licensed and board certified, the number of years since the medical degree was conferred, whether the doctor or other provider is certified in her respective specialty field, affiliation with at least one professional society related to their specialty, and the number of malpractice lawsuits and disciplinary actions taken against them.

Learn to Communicate with Providers

Who doesn't know how to communicate? You do it all day every day—with partners, children, employees, even with the guy who runs the cash register at the fast-food restaurant. Unfortunately, communicating with providers is not nearly as cut and dry. Specific intentions need to be laid out in order to communicate effectively. You also must be an active listener, which means truly seeking to understand what the other person is saying and being aware of any barriers that may keep you from hearing what the other person has to say.

Begin with the assumption that everyone you encounter on the journey to healing your child's eating disorder has your family's best interests at heart. That may not mean you agree with every recommendation, but it does put you both on the same side.

Know What Is Needed

One of the keys to communicating with providers is to prepare ahead of time so you know what you hope to attain from the visit. Do you need a referral, lab testing, or a prescription review? Each requires a different way of thinking, and knowing that puts you in the driver's seat as a health care consumer. That doesn't mean you aren't open to other possibilities, suggestions, or alternatives, but it means that you walk into every single appointment with a clear understanding of what your child needs, knowing what you want from each appointment, and clearly stating your expectations with the health care provider. It also means being able to speak up when those needs are not being met to your satisfaction.

Be Patient, Polite, and Persistent

If your child is having a medical crisis, then being patient and polite is irrelevant. That being said, as a general rule, when you are communicating with your child's providers, being patient, polite, and persistent is key. Realize your health care providers are not infallible. Most of them genuinely want to help but may not have the ability, knowledge base, or time to do so. If anyone is ever rude, insensitive, uninformative, or generally unhelpful, that provider is not for you and it is okay to move on.

 Essential

Consider what you're saying through your nonverbal communication. Your volume, tone, facial expression, and body language all convey powerful messages. If your words say one thing and your body says another, your mixed messages may not get the response you're seeking.

When You Disagree

It is not necessarily a disaster if you disagree with a health care provider. If someone asks you to make a decision with which you are not comfortable, it is perfectly appropriate to repeat back what you understand was said and then ask any questions you might have on the provider's perspective. Unless your child is having a medical emergency, an immediate decision rarely needs to be made. You can thank the provider for his time and let him know that you will consider his perspective and seek to make the best decision for your child after considering all options. If you disagree vehemently and have no intention of considering the offered suggestion, you can still thank the person for his or her time and state your own opinion as you feel necessary without screaming, accusations, or sarcasm.

It's Not Me, It's You

As your child's advocate, remember that you "hire" the health care provider every time you go in for a visit. As such, you can choose to "fire" the provider any time you wish if you no longer believe that he or she is the best fit for your needs. You are paying for the provider's time and expertise, and you have the right to ask any health care provider you see what his or her background and experience is. If you don't understand the answer to a question, ask the doctor to explain it again until you do understand it. If he becomes exasperated and frustrated with your questions or expectations, then you may need to move on to a different provider.

 Fact

Be honest about your financial situation. If your doctor prescribes medicine you can't afford, talk about it and ask for an alternative medication or other option.

Not Welcome Here

There are times you may have a health care provider who, whether for physical or mental health concerns, will not welcome your active participation in the care and treatment of your child. Indications that your provider will not encourage or even allow your involvement include professionals who:

- Advise parents to leave treatment decisions, including nutritional and weight decisions, to children
- Advise parents not to discuss treatment and not involve parents in the treatment
- Advise parents not to be the "food police" or be involved with cooking and food decisions
- Advise parents that patients have to "want" to get better
- Regard parent responsibilities around this illness as distinct from those with other serious illnesses

Take Care of the Details

Consider your child's eating disorder treatment as your new part-time job. At times, it may become your full-time job. Just as in any job, keeping track of the details is critical to operational success. The same is true for your child's eating disorder treatment. Document everything. Keep all bills and receipts, and write down names of specialists visited, treatments undergone, and dates of visits. If you talk to your insurance provider, write down who you talked to, when, and what about. Keep copies of all test and lab results. Maintaining insurance records, doctor's appointments, prescription information, and reactions are all important.

Create Your Notebook

Start your own binder specifically for your child's eating disorder treatment. Divide it into several sections that you think will best work for you. You may want to consider having sections on:

- Daily/weekly status notes
- Contact information for team members
- Lab results
- Treatment notes
- Medication records, including current medications and dosages, any side effects, and medications that have been discontinued
- Health insurance forms, numbers, and bills
- Questions to ask

Make sure your team members have copies of appropriate information, prescription medications, lab tests, and any other test results or medical information (what treatments worked, what didn't work, family history, allergies, etc.) you can give them. The more history that doctors know, the better they can help.

I'll Take a Copy

One of the important parts of your binder are the reports and test results from health care providers. You need a copy of the results of every test that is done, whether psychological or medical.

You are probably familiar with HIPAA if you've been to a doctor in the past several years. HIPAA stands for Health Insurance Portability and Accountability Act, which was signed into law in 1996 (Public Law 104-191) and governs medical records. You may be used to seeing notices that discuss how your medical records will be used, but the law also gives you access to your medical records. The law gives you the right to see your and your child's medical records while you are in your doctor's office. Parents of minor children have access to their child's medical records, as long as it is consistent with any other state and other governing law.

 Essential

Never sign something you don't know or understand. If you don't understand something, find someone you trust who can make sense of things and advise you accordingly.

The law also requires your doctor to give a copy of your medical records to you, although the doctor has up to thirty days to do so. The physician may extend that deadline for another month but must provide a reason for the delay. You may be charged a reasonable fee for copying the file, but the fee may only include the cost of copying (including supplies and labor) and postage if the patient requests that the copy be mailed. The only other allowable fees are if the patient (or patient's legal guardian) requests a summary or explanation of the records, and the preparer may charge a fee for that service.

If you wish to get a copy of your child's medical records, it is not appropriate to walk up to the receptionist at the front desk and ask. Instead, you should request a copy of the office's medical records release form. It should be fully filled out then faxed or mailed to the appropriate address. If you are not confident the request will be met in a timely manner, you may wish to send the form certified mail so a signature is required and you have proof your letter was received.

If you find a mistake, you can request that the medical record be corrected or amended to add information if the file is incomplete. If your doctor agrees there was an error in the records, such as an incorrect medication name, then the record must be changed. If the doctor doesn't agree, you still have the right to have your disagreement noted in your child's medical records. Generally, the file should be changed within two months.

Cheat Sheet

Keep a quick reference medicine chart with you and your child at all times. In the case of an emergency or a new physician appointment, you will have at your fingertips a list of your child's medications, allergies, diagnoses, and blood type. You can hand it to the medical provider even when emotions are running high without having to worry about forgetting something important.

Write a Letter

Depending on the situation, you may need to write letters regarding your child's eating disorder. Whether it is to a health care provider, health insurance company, or school system, having a record of your requests or concerns provides additional protection if problems arise down the road. When you send a letter, always keep a copy for your records. When asking for something specific, request a response within a certain time frame and provide information on ways that you can be reached. Keep hard copies of all correspondence.

 Essential

Before you send a letter, put it away for a day or two and then reread it with fresh eyes, or ask a friend or family member to read it to confirm that your request is clear, respectful, and includes necessary facts.

Your records of past requests, denial letters, and benefit explanations will allow you to stay organized, document needs, and help you achieve your desired results.

Connect with Others

Connecting with other people who have similar experiences can be an important part of being an active and visible presence in the care of your child. Sometimes, in the midst of coping with your child's eating disorder, you just feel stuck. You may feel as though you are completely out of resources, that you don't have any more options, and that your particular situation feels hopeless. That is the time, more than ever, you need to hear from those who are a few steps ahead of you on the path.

Advocacy Organizations

There are many organizations that are dedicated to providing information, support, and protecting the rights of people with eating disorders. Advocacy organizations can offer valuable tools for parents, teachers, and others by:

- Teaching advocacy skills
- Providing accurate information for families
- Offering resources for families to share with others
- Speaking out about health issues that families face individually and collectively
- Fighting against insurance companies who deny treatment for people with eating disorders

Online Forums

If you have never been to a support group or online forum for parents whose children are suffering from an eating disorder, then you are depriving yourself of a significant source of not only emotional support but also of information. Eileen, a mother of a child with an eating disorder, admits, "I was very resistant to speaking with other parents because, frankly, I have enough of my own battles. I don't need to wallow in anyone else's misery. I expected everyone I spoke with to be gloom and doom and crying all the time. What I didn't realize was that it was possible to laugh, even in the midst of this. Plus, I got tons of encouragement, ideas, and sometimes even a kick in the pants when I was the one who was glooming and dooming."

Fact

Not sure what websites you can trust for accurate health information? Look for the Health on the Net (HON) badge. It grants its badge to health websites that meet its strict criteria, including privacy, transparency, attribution, and authority. For more information, check out *www.hon.ch.*

Some guidelines for getting the most out of online forums:

- Protect your anonymity, and do not use personal information that could potentially allow someone to identify you.
- Start low and go slow. Once you have participated in a forum, you'll be better able to discern who is the most knowledgeable and who is (or isn't) a safe resource.
- Participate and offer support to other families. It can be empowering to share information, resources, and encouragement with others.
- Open your mind. People will come to the forums from a wide variety of experiences, cultures, backgrounds, and perspectives. Don't expect everyone else—or even anyone else—to have the exact same point of view that you do. That doesn't mean, however, that you can't learn from other participants.
- Verify any information before acting on it. Whether it's a medication or treatment approach, don't make any treatment decisions without doing due diligence first.

No Room for Fear

An often unspoken part of becoming an advocate is the ability to recognize and, on some level, live with the very real fear involved in accepting responsibility for a child's health care. The most common mistakes that parents make when dealing with their child's eating disorder is not doing anything because they are afraid of making the situation worse. You can't make it worse by addressing it. You can only make it worse by ignoring it.

School Issues

It is possible that your child's eating disorder will affect your child's education. In an emergent situation, your child might need long-term residential treatment, a short-term hospital stay, an intensive outpatient program, or even just multiple doctor appointments during the school day. Your child's school may need to make accommodations, and it will be important to communicate with appropriate school authorities. If possible, you may want to request an academic team meeting so that you can speak directly to all of your child's teachers and administrative staff as necessary.

Keep in mind that the school staff may have outdated beliefs about eating disorders, its cause, and treatment, and you may have to provide education as a part of the process. Ideally, you can ask for a main contact person at the school to work with to establish an ongoing system of communication. This may be a school guidance counselor, teacher, or administrator.

Develop a Thick Skin

If you're waiting for your child to kneel on the ground in gratitude for your wisdom and graciousness in coping with her eating disorder, you might have to wait a while. She probably won't express any gratitude, at least for a very long time. The disease is a tenacious one and doesn't give up easily. Being your child's advocate may well mean making choices that your child vehemently disagrees with, as do other family members, friends, and even professionals. If you are prepared for such criticism, then it won't be as likely to blindside you and you can take it in stride.

Focus on Short-Term Goals

When your child was an infant, he made developmental steps in increments. When he was learning to walk, he crawled first then cruised around the table, then took baby steps and fell down and got back up. He didn't just wake up one morning and decide that this was the day he was going to walk. Recovery is a lot like that. Your child won't wake up tomorrow and embrace the eating disorder recovery. That's okay. Advocating for your child means that you keep the big picture in mind, even when your child seems to stop moving forward or may even take a step back.

Sticks and Stones

Almost as long as eating disorders have been identified, parents have been vilified. When empowered parents become the decision-makers in their child's eating disorder treatment, they may need to prepare themselves for criticism. Such parents may face professionals who believe that parents should be seen and not heard; they may even be told that their involvement represents a barrier to their child's autonomy. As a parent advocate, you are loving, well-intentioned, supportive, and uniquely capable of helping your child.

Oversee your child's health care. From the financial aspects such as billing overcharges to the potentially dangerous such as knowing drug interactions, only you can see the whole picture and connect the dots to limit risks and surprises. Being an advocate boils down to taking an active role in your family's health care. Working with your doctors and other health care members to create a plan that you understand and that works for you will not protect your child from the eating disorder, but you can follow a plan to achieve the goals you helped set.

CHAPTER 9

Paying for Treatment

In what seems like adding insult to injury, parents not only have to find the most appropriate treatment for their child, they also need to find a way to pay for it. It is possible that a significant amount of medical and psychological care may be needed in caring for your child. As such, effectively treating an eating disorder can be a long and expensive endeavor.

The Costs of Treatment

In an ideal world, you could quickly and easily access the best, most effective treatment for your child regardless of the cost. The good news is that evidence-based treatment recommendations suggest that in-home care is ideal for most children with eating disorders. That does not, however, mean that your child would not need medical hospitalization or residential care. How you are going to pay for treatment for your child's eating disorder treatment is, unfortunately, one of the primary factors that you have to consider when choosing her care.

Inpatient Care

Treatment of an eating disorder in the United States ranges from $500 to $2,000 per day for inpatient care. The average cost for a month of inpatient treatment is $30,000. Some centers are much higher, while others are much less expensive. It is estimated that individuals with eating disorders need anywhere from three to six months of inpatient care. Health insurance companies, for several reasons, do not typically cover the costs of treating eating disorders in residential facilities, but some do.

Outpatient Care

The cost of outpatient treatment, including therapy and medical monitoring, can extend to $100,000 or more. What makes outpatient care so expensive? Physician appointments, lab work, medications, and therapy can become prohibitively expensive. In a given week of eating disorder treatment, a child may have one to two counseling sessions, medications, and a psychiatrist or physician appointment. Depending on the part of the country in which you live, costs can vary significantly. In Indianapolis, for example, the average cost of a psychiatrist visit is $125, while the average fee in larger metropolitan cities often tops $200.

What If You Don't Have Health Insurance?

Too often, parents assume that they have no options for eating disorder treatment if they do not have health insurance. Not having health insurance is difficult and will likely involve a considerable expenditure of time and energy to locate appropriate resources. That being said, it does not mean that you are without help.

Local Resources

Most public schools have a social worker who is familiar with community health and mental health resources. If your child is in college, most colleges have nurses and counselors on staff who can provide at least rudimentary support and who should be familiar with local resources.

Federal Programs

Medicaid is the largest source of funding for medical and health-related services for people with limited incomes. More than 40 million people have Medicaid coverage, and about half are children. In order to be approved and receive the funding, certain eligibility requirements must be met. Go to *www.cms.gov* to look up eligibility requirements for your state.

Even if you think you don't qualify for Medicaid services because your income might be too high, check out the Medicaid website (*www.cms.gov/MedicaidStWaivProgDemoPGI/*) for waiver programs (meaning the income requirements are waived) in your state. States are somewhat flexible in how they spend Medicaid money, and you may be able to enroll your child in a Medicaid waiver program that will help with crisis management, intensive in-home support, parent advocacy, and more.

State Health Coverage

Each state in the United States has a health program for children who come from low-income families. Under the Children's Health Insurance Plan (CHIP), each qualified child whose family income is under its income requirement bracket is either covered for free or is given low-cost insurance. For more information on CHIP, contact your state's health department.

 Fact

If your child needs emergency medical treatment and you do not have health insurance, it is against the law for a hospital to refuse treatment to your child. When your child is stabilized, a hospital may transfer your child to another facility, but it cannot refuse to treat your child.

Cobra Coverage

If you lose your job that provided health insurance coverage for your family, you may be able to maintain your coverage through COBRA, or the Consolidated Omnibus Budget Reconciliation Act. It gives workers and their families who lose their health benefits the ability to continue group health benefits provided by their group health plan for limited periods of time under certain circumstances such as job loss (voluntary or involuntary), reduction in the hours worked, transition between jobs, death, divorce, and other life events.

Unfortunately, the costs can often be prohibitive, as employers are not required to pay the portion of the fees that they covered during full employment. The federal laws regarding COBRA are often in flux, so you will need to check for the most recent laws affecting COBRA coverage. You can find more information on COBRA at the U.S. Department of Labor website: *www.dol.gov/dol/topic/health-plans/cobra.htm*.

How to Tell What's Covered

For many parents, getting treatment related to their child's eating disorder may be the first time they have had to deal with their health insurance company in a meaningful way. You need to understand if your health insurance includes coverage for mental health services, the types of services that are covered, and the amount paid for these services, as well as any steps you must take to have treatment covered.

The Fine Print

The first step to understanding your health insurance is to read through the Summary Plan Description that you received when your insurance started. If you only have the one- or two-page summary of benefits, then you do not have all the paperwork you need. This short document may be easy to understand, but it is not the legal document that would be used if a dispute ends up in court. For a complete description of your plan's benefits, contact your employer's human resources department for a copy of what is known as the Evidence of Coverage or Certificate of Coverage.

 **Question**

Are there safe ways I can cut costs?
When your child needs blood work or other tests, see if there is a local laboratory that can do the same tests for less money. It's possible to save hundreds of dollars on diagnostic tests just by shopping around.

The plan is updated regularly, so you need the most up-to-date policy. In the plan description, the section titled Benefits is usually broken down into five parts: medical/surgery, prescription drugs, extended care, emergency care, and mental health.

The Name Game

Part of what becomes tricky when dealing with health insurance and eating disorders is where the treatment falls. Is it covered under medical care or under mental health?

Besides knowing what coverage you have, you need to know which covered treatments are funded through the health section of your plan and which are funded through mental health services. This is another reason why getting a thorough physical and mental health assessment is critical.

Often there are coexisting medical and emotional issues beyond the eating disorder. It is not unusual for children and teens with eating disorders to be diagnosed with any number of other disorders, including depression, trauma, obsessive-compulsive disorder, anxiety, social phobias, and chemical dependence. While it may seem overwhelming to have yet another diagnosis, coexisting conditions can affect your child's eligibility for various benefits.

It is generally to your advantage to keep medical services funded through the medical section of your plan. For example, if your son's psychiatrist is providing medication management services, utilize your medical coverage because there is often a lower copay and services are not as limited.

Get It in Writing

Even if you get approval for coverage during a telephone call with a representative from your health insurance provider, it won't stand up in court. An insurance company can deny a claim once the bill has been turned in even if you called and got approval first. Although it can still happen, it is much more difficult for an insurance company to deny a claim if you have a precertifying letter.

 Essential

Say "thank you" and compliment anyone who helps you, even if it is his or her job to do so. Remember, you are much more likely to receive friendly service when you are respectful and polite while still being persistent.

The National Eating Disorders Association has sample letters that you can send to the insurance company requesting precertification for treatment. You must send all letters certified mail so that you have confirmation they were received. Keep in mind that the postal service won't deliver certified letters to PO boxes. The mailing address in your benefits book should be listed in the section on appeals.

When Your Claim Is Denied

Because treating eating disorders can be very expensive, health insurers are going to be reluctant to pay, even if they are supposed to do so. As many as one-fifth of all legitimate claims are thought to be denied by insurance companies. After all, the more services the insurance company pays for, the less profit the insurance company makes. It is possible that your health insurance should cover care for your child with an eating disorder and still turn down your request.

If your claim is denied, the next step is to ask for a written explanation. Most states require insurance companies to provide such a written explanation, and failure to do so may constitute an illegal practice. Your written denial will also include information on how many days you have to file an appeal, should you choose to do so.

The most common reasons that your claim is denied include:

- Your plan says the health care service or item you want covered is not medically necessary
- You did not get a prior authorization before you got the health care service or item, and your plan says you needed one.
- You want to use an out-of-network doctor or other provider
- You did not get a referral from your doctor
- Your plan says the health care service or item is not a covered by your plan

Determining Grounds for Appeal

Your health insurance plan will spell out in detail what your options are to go through an appeals process. To file an appeal, you must find out what the internal process is for your health plan. Some companies will allow you to file an appeal electronically via e-mail or a form on the company website, or through a company telephone number. While those methods may seem more convenient than an actual letter, a physical letter can be verified in ways that a telephone call cannot be.

If an insurance company denies your claim for coverage and you believe they were wrong in doing so, then you may have grounds for an appeal. Remember, it is a waste of time to file an appeal claim if your insurance policy specifically excludes eating disorder treatment and your claim specifies eating disorder treatment only and not any co-current psychiatric problems such as depression or anxiety. Read the denial letter carefully, as sometimes the denial letter will quote your policy incorrectly.

 Essential

If your health insurance coverage is provided through your employer and you are experiencing unreasonable delays or denials, then contact your company's benefits administrator for assistance. He may prove to be a valuable advocate on your behalf.

If the insurance company denies a claim because you filed a form incorrectly or past a deadline, an insurance company cannot refuse to pay an otherwise valid claim unless the company can show it has been harmed by your error or prevented from making an adequate investigation due to your delay.

And Another Appeal

Even if your claim is denied for a second time, the denial letter will tell you what your options are for a second appeal. Again, the denial letter should specify why your claim was denied and how many days you have to appeal. Look at why your claim was denied and talk to your health care provider about suggestions for having the decision reversed. Ask your health care provider to be on the conference call for the next hearing.

You have the right to hire a professional arbitrator or an attorney to battle your insurance company on your behalf, but fees can add up quickly.

If you have filed appeals and you are not satisfied with the results, the state commissioner may help. If you need assistance with a claim against your insurance company, you can contact the insurance commission in your state. To find the contact information, go to the National Association of Insurance Commissioners at *www .naic.org* or call 816-842-3600. However, your state's insurance commissioner cannot:

- Act as your legal representative or give you legal advice
- Recommend insurance companies or HMOs
- Force a company to give you what you want if no laws have been broken
- Make determinations about medical necessity
- Address problems with your employer's health plan

If your second appeal was denied, you may still have the option of requesting an external appeal. In this type of appeal, a person who does not work for your insurance company is the one who makes the decision, and this time it is final. An external appeal is typically done via telephone conference call.

When Not to Appeal

There are times when it is not worth your time and energy to launch an appeal against your insurance company. If your health insurance company denies your claim wrongly, then, by all means, appeal. In other words, if your policy book says such services are covered and they won't cover the services, keep up the fight. But if the insurance booklet clearly states that such services are not covered, then the company is not legally bound to do so.

 Essential

The Family and Medical Leave Act (FMLA) allows eligible employees to take off up to twelve work weeks in any twelve-month period to care for an ill family member. While it is generally unpaid, you cannot be fired from your position for taking time off to care for your child. There are a number of limitations; to determine your eligibility, go to the Department of Labor's website at *www.dol.gov/whd/fmla/*.

You might correctly believe that your insurance company should be morally bound to provide services for your child, but, unfortunately, that is irrelevant to most insurance companies. They will only provide coverage for services they are legally obligated to cover. That means regardless of how many pictures or compelling letters you send, they aren't going to change their mind. In this situation, you may need to direct your focus toward finding resources that are available to you and your child given your current situation.

Where Do You Live?

Find out if your state has a mental health parity law. Mental health parity means that your health insurance company is not allowed to limit mental health and substance abuse health care by imposing lower day and visit limits, higher copayments and deductibles, and lower annual and lifetime spending caps. The Center for Mental Health Services report on state parity laws at *http://store .samhsa.gov/product/SMA07-4228* provides state-specific information about mental health parity.

Alternate Avenues

If you don't have health insurance, the insurance company turns you down again, or you aren't eligible for state or federal programs, there are still some other options for accessing appropriate care for your child.

Working with the Health Care Provider

Health care providers who care for people with eating disorders understand the difficulties involved with insurance companies and often have a staff member dedicated to helping you solve insurance problems. If your health care provider assists you in writing an appeal, they must use the language of your policy in their letter.

Fact

Check out updates from the Eating Disorder Coalition (*www.eating disorderscoalition.org*), a nonprofit organization working to improve access to eating disorder treatment by advancing the federal recognition of eating disorders as a public health priority.

Most therapists' or doctors' offices do not routinely bill or extend credit, and they expect full payment for services rendered at each visit. If you have health insurance, the front office will often confirm what your insurance company will pay and let you know what your estimated payment will be. Should insurance pay a different amount than what the office anticipates, they will usually bill you. Otherwise, offices usually accept cash, check, credit cards, as well as any in-house finance programs.

 Essential

If your child is in college, many college campuses have on-campus counselors, health centers, and support groups focused on helping students access mental health care services. Typically, programs are free or low cost.

It may be possible to negotiate a lower rate with your health care provider for paying in cash. If a lower rate is not possible, perhaps paying in installments is an option. Be honest about your financial and insurance situation and ask for any input or suggestions they might have to offer. You are not the first patient they have had who has dealt with financial concerns. You are more likely to be successful if you work with an independent contractor and not a provider operating from within a large hospital network. An independent provider typically has more latitude regarding billing policies.

Go Green

Using less experienced therapists, medical doctors, or psychiatrists can also be a way to save money. Sometimes counselors under supervision will charge up to 50 percent less than more experienced counselors. In the same way, medical care at teaching hospitals may prove to be more affordable.

 Essential

Clinical studies are another option for free or low-cost medical or psychiatric care. Go to *www.clinicaltrials.gov* for a searchable database that provides patients, family members, and the public with information about current ongoing *clinical* research studies.

While you may be initially hesitant about using less experienced providers, remember that they are most often working under the supervision of more experienced staff (but ask to make sure), and they are more likely to be aware of and use the most up-to-date research on eating disorder treatment.

Eating Disorder Treatment Programs

A common mistake that some parents make is assuming that the treatment they think their child needs is not an option due to prohibitive costs. While some eating disorder treatment programs are for-profit companies, not all are. Almost all residential treatment programs in the United States have a dedicated staff member focused on maximizing health insurance benefits and working with families to help facilitate treatment.

Nonprofit Organizations

There are a handful of nonprofit organizations that are dedicated to providing financial support to people who need eating disorder treatment but do not have the financial means to do so.

🅔❗ Alert

The organizations' ability to fund services vary, but here are several organizations that may be able to offer financial support and can provide additional information on financial resources:

- Mercy Ministries (*www.mercyministries.org*)
- Milestones in Recovery (*www.milestonesprogram.org*)
- Be Totally Free (*www.thenelsoncenter.com*)
- Renfrew Center Foundation (*www.renfrew.org*)
- Eating Disorder Referral and Information Center (*www.edreferral.com/scholarship_foundation.htm*)
- SAMHSA's National Mental Health Information Center (*http://store.samhsa.gov/home*)
- The Gail R. Schoenbach Foundation for Recovery and Elimination of Eating Disorders (*www.freedfoundation.org*)

CHAPTER 10

Understanding Treatment Options

Type "eating disorder treatment" in a search engine and you'll get over a million hits. Where do you begin? Now that you know the severity of your child's illness, the next step is to learn what treatment options are right for your family and for your child. Sadly, just as there aren't easy answers to what caused your child's eating disorder, finding the solution isn't the easiest process, either. The right treatment mix will likely have multiple components and may take months to assemble.

What Treatment Means

With treatment, the mortality rate from eating disorders falls to 2 to 3 percent. While those numbers aren't ideal, they are good news. The vast majority of people who are treated for an eating disorder will recover fully and completely. Treatment for an eating disorder is often multifaceted and may require medication and supportive counseling.

Individual Treatment Plan

There will be multiple opportunities to make treatment decisions when your child has an eating disorder. What you will need to look for in a treatment team is one that will allow you to collaboratively create a treatment plan that is designed specifically for your child. An individual treatment plan is the master plan that outlines and defines the course of treatment for your child. It is a comprehensive and holistic plan that delineates the goals, objectives, resources, and main team members of the treatment process. It should also be a living document; that is, it can be fluid and change as your child's needs change. The problem is that every treatment center says that is exactly what they will do, but that's not always the case. According to Chris Hanson, in the *Eating Disorder Survival Guide*, here are some goals that your treatment plan and team should strive to put in place:

- Eating should be guided by physical hunger and not emotional hunger
- Your child recognizes and responds to hunger as a guide for eating appropriately
- In females, menstruation is restored and maintained without the need for oral contraceptives
- Healthy body composition with lean body mass and body fat is restored and maintained. This is different from a specific body weight or even a BMI.
- Purging behavior, diet pills, laxative use, and excessive exercise is absent
- Patient will tolerate a wide variety of high-quality foods in a well-balanced diet so that protein, carbohydrates, fatty acids, minerals, and vitamins are consumed
- Your child can tolerate "spontaneous" natural eating
- Significant decrease in amount of time spent obsessing about weight, food, and/or body image, while the ability to cope without using disordered eating is increased

 **Essential**

You do not need to ever settle for treatment that isn't working, is stalled, settles for less than 100 percent recovery, or stops before the patient is fully self-sufficient. It is important for parents to know that full physical, emotional, and cognitive recovery is not rare, nor is it unattainable. If properly treated, an eating disorder can be limited in duration and does not have to cause long-term medical consequences.

Food Is Medicine

There are professionals who will act as though the food piece of eating disorder treatment is incidental. They are wrong. The malnourished brain cannot think clearly and logically. The initial focus of recovery must be on restoring full nutrition. Only when the child is no longer suffering from malnutrition can the work of healthy thinking begin.

Levels of Care Determination

There are five levels of care that correspond with the various needs of eating disorder patients, according to the American Psychiatric Association. Level one is outpatient treatment, generally when a patient is at 85 percent or more of ideal weight. Level two is intensive outpatient treatment and is designed for a patient at 80 percent or higher of ideal weight. Level three is partial hospitalization (full-day outpatient care). Level four is residential treatment center, and patients in the level four category are medically stable to the extent that they do not require intravenous fluids, tube feedings, or multiple daily laboratory tests. Level five is inpatient hospitalization. These specific levels of care are not often used other than for insurance purposes.

Setting Treatment Goals

If your child had type 1 diabetes, you would know the disease was being managed appropriately when the blood sugar was at a healthy level. Blood work would provide a picture of overall disease management. There is no such test when your child has an eating disorder. That makes it difficult to know when treatment is effective and when it can be completed. There are, however, several indicators that can suggest whether or not treatment is effective.

Restore to a Healthy Weight

Particularly for those with anorexia and binge eating disorder, restoration to a healthy weight can be one indicator of health. However, increasing or decreasing weight can take a significant amount of time; consequently, failure to progress may take time to identify.

Inpatient Care

There are times when a child's eating disorder is so severe or so persistent that the best treatment option is inpatient care, either in a hospital setting or in a residential treatment center. Deciding if or when inpatient treatment is appropriate is not an easy decision.

Medical Hospitalization

Few hospitals have the ability to deal with children and teenagers with eating disorders. Larger hospitals may have psychiatric units for children and teens, but few are equipped with eating disorder specialists. However, inpatient hospital care may be appropriate when your child's health is at immediate risk. If your child weighs less than 75 percent of normal body weight, then inpatient care may be necessary to provide intravenous fluid and electrolytes.

Residential Treatment

Residential treatment programs typically have a residential or campus-type setting, and they provide much of the structure that inpatient hospital programs provide but are not intended for persons whose health is severely compromised. Persons in this category may weigh less than 85 percent but more than 75 percent of normal body weight.

Partial Hospitalization

In partial hospitalization, clients attend hospital facility activities such as group therapy and didactic groups during the day but retreat to either their homes or residential-type facilities at the end of the day. Partial hospitalization or day hospital programs may run four to seven days per week.

Partial hospitalization patients benefit from the same basic treatment options that inpatient persons receive only without the extended medical supervision. In many treatment center programs, inpatient persons regularly transition to partial hospitalization after they have demonstrated a certain level of recovery. Partial hospitalization patients are generally responsible for preparing their own breakfasts and dinners, whereas inpatient persons have all meals served to them. The stepped-down level of care in partial hospitalization affords clients the responsibility to move toward increasing self-nurturance and, thus, greater emotional and physical health.

Nutritional Goals

There is no set nutritional rehabilitation goal for all eating disorder patients. Not every person needs the same amount of calories, even those who need to gain or lose weight. As such, an effective nutritional treatment plan will be personalized for the needs of each person. Nutritional treatment often involves education regarding the perception of "good" and "bad" foods, what a healthy diet looks like, and learning to face specific food fears.

Anorexia

The American Psychiatric Association has suggested a target weight gain for persons with anorexia at two to three pounds per week. Correspondingly, meal planning for anorexia nervosa patients should begin with 1,000 to 1,600 calories per day, which may be increased by 70 to 100 calories per day during the weight gain phase of treatment. In a medical setting, if the food is not eaten, then the patient may be offered an opportunity to consume the remaining calories in a supplemental beverage, and if that is refused, then a nasal gastric (NG) tube may be offered.

Bulimia

Nutritional rehabilitation for people with bulimia, who are frequently of average weight, does not usually include weight gain. Nutritional counseling best serves many persons with bulimia in the form of behavioral reduction and, eventually, eradication regarding binging, purging, and food restriction, according to the American Psychiatric Association.

Binge Eating Disorder

Binge eating disorder nutrition treatment focuses on creating a pattern of eating healthy meals at regular intervals. Patients may practice eating a small amount of a food they may have binged on and look for ways to cope with unhealthy thinking patterns without using food to do so.

When Hospitalization Is Necessary

Sometimes, the most appropriate treatment for a child with an eating disorder is immediate hospitalization. A child cannot begin the process of recovery if there isn't some physical stability. Indications for hospitalization in children will vary. Each health insurance company will have its own criteria for hospitalization, and you can expect their hospitalization guidelines to be fairly strict and may, in fact, put your child's health at risk. In particular, children with EDNOS or bulimia, for example, may not meet insurance guidelines for hospitalization but may still require inpatient care.

Indications for Hospitalization for Anorexia Nervosa

Some indications that a child needs to be hospitalized include:

- Weight loss continues, even with outpatient treatment.
- Weight is 30 percent below ideal body weight.
- Depression is extreme or he or she is suicidal.
- Symptoms of medical complications indicate the need; for example, a disturbed heart rate, altered mental status, low potassium levels, and low blood pressure all indicate a need for inpatient care.

Indications for Hospitalization for Bulimia Nervosa

Some indications that a child with bulimia may need to be hospitalized include:

- Changes in vital signs (pulse, blood pressure)
- Syncope, or fainting
- Hypothermia
- Suicide risk
- Alcohol or drug abuse
- Uncontrolled vomiting
- Hematemesis (vomiting of blood)
- Arrhythmia
- Electrolyte imbalance
- Need for withdrawal from laxatives, diet pills, and diuretics

This list is not all-inclusive, and there may be other indicators for hospitalization, although it can be difficult to get health insurance approval for a child with bulimia, especially if his or her weight is at a "normal" level.

Hospitalization for Other Eating Disorders

If your child has EDNOS or binge eating disorder, it may be very difficult to get health insurance approval for hospitalization. Often one of the only ways that a child is admitted is for severe dehydration, depression, or if there is a suicide risk. While binge eating disorder does have health risks, the risks tend to be long term and typically do not put a child at immediate health risk.

Hospital Admission

A child is usually admitted through the emergency room or directly onto a floor if being admitted by a physician. A parent will need to take care of insurance paperwork and other admission requirements while the child has an initial assessment. How and when that happens depends on how the child is admitted. Bring pertinent medical information with you, including the names and contact number of all health care providers, medications, allergies, and recent lab tests.

Lab Work

Typically, new admissions are given an identification tag, and a lab technician may come in to draw blood for a complete blood count, or CBC. If your child is very thin or dehydrated, it may be difficult to find a vein. If the lab tech is not successful on the first or second stick, it is appropriate to tell the lab person to stop and find another who may be more experienced. It is important that blood is drawn so the electrolyte levels can be carefully monitored. An intravenous (IV) line may also be inserted early in the admission. An IV line allows for the easy insertion of medicine and fluids directly into your child's bloodstream. Medication works faster through an intravenous line than when it is given orally. An IV line is generally kept in throughout the entire hospital stay.

 **Question**

If my child has a medical condition, why is he being placed on a psychiatric unit?
Most children and teens with an ED will be placed on a psychiatric unit unless there is a severe medical crisis. Some researchers and many parents believe that because an eating disorder is a medical illness, it should be treated as such in the hospital setting. However, resisting such placement can be very difficult.

Forced Nutrition

"We had our regularly scheduled meeting with a physician who is a specialist in eating disorders and he told us that our son had to be hospitalized. His weight had just gotten too low. He was at a dangerous level. We needed to have him admitted and we need to do it tonight. When we got to the hospital, the first thing they did was put him on a feeding tube because they wanted to stabilize his weight," explains Paul, whose son was on a feeding tube for over a week. "We just didn't expect it and didn't expect his reaction to it."

One of the fastest ways to stabilize a person with an eating disorder is to put in a feeding tube. A feeding tube, medically known as a percutaneous endoscopic gastrostomy (PEG), is inserted through one of the nostrils, down through the back of the throat, through the esophagus, and into the stomach. Being fed through a PEG is also known as *gavage*, enteral feeding, or tube feeding. The criteria for placing a feeding tube varies by physician, but it is typically called for when one or more of these criteria are met:

- The patient is less than or equal to 85 percent ideal body weight (IBW).
- The patient has experienced greater than one month severe restriction (less than 500 calories per day) prior to admission.
- A three-day calorie count reveals intake below maintenance/gain calories.

- The patient is severely restricting fluid intake and needs the NG tube to maintain hydration status.

Only a physician or registered nurse can insert a feeding tube, and while it isn't painful, it isn't comfortable, either. Your child will probably gag as it is being placed. Fortunately, it doesn't take long to insert, as long as the patient cooperates, and once it is in place, it is taped to the nose and left in.

 Essential

Taking small sips of water can help get the feeding tube to a comfortable location. If the health care provider does not offer, ask if your child can have water. If no fluids are allowed, then swallowing should aid in tube placement. A feeding tube is only meant to be a short-term solution to a long-term problem. Tube feedings are meant to stabilize a child in crisis and will not remedy the larger issue.

When Your Child Won't Cooperate

"My daughter wouldn't eat at home. We sat for hours at the table and she could not take a bite of food. She knew that our only other option was to go to the hospital. I packed her up, took her in, and the nursing staff gave her a choice: she had thirty minutes to eat the meal, and if she didn't, then she would receive the same number of calories in a beverage. Again, she had thirty minutes to drink all of it. Whatever was left at that time would be inserted into her stomach via a nasal gastric tube. She refused the food, and then at the end of twenty minutes she saw another girl who refused her drink get an NG tube and it scared her. She downed her drink in no time."

As a child with an eating disorder is clearly not thinking clearly, it is likely that she will be less than thrilled with these more extreme measures. In fact, your child may actively resist the tube feeding or intravenous line, either refusing to cooperate during insertion or by forcible removing once the lines are in place. When that happens, your child's physician will be forced to make a decision about what to do. If the feeding or fluids is deemed to be critical in protecting your child's health, then the physician may order that your child's wrists and ankles be restrained so she cannot do further harm.

If there are consequences that are clearly spelled out, a staff person should speak with your child and let him or her know what the potential consequences are going to be. The possibility of being restrained may be enough to encourage a reluctant, but voluntary, acceptance. If your child requires inpatient care, parents will generally receive an inpatient packet, particularly when the child is placed on a psychiatric unit. The packet will typically include guidelines regarding the use of restraints. Restraints can be physical, where someone holds down your child, or mechanical, where straps are used. Chemical restraints can also be used, which means that a medication is used to calm the child.

If your child is placed in restraints, the following should occur:

- You should be informed immediately why restraint of your child is needed. A parent's informed consent is always preferred and sometimes is required before restraints are administered.
- You should be informed of ways that you can be supportive, including helping your child understand how to avoid it occurring in the future.
- You may be asked to act as a sitter to help prevent problematic behaviors. You should be involved in the discussion that takes place after the use of restraints.

Discharged Does Not Mean Cured

One of the most common mistakes parents make after their child has been hospitalized is to think that the eating disorder has been resolved. It hasn't been. Your child has been released from the hospital because she is out of immediate danger, or because your health insurance has decided it will not longer pay for inpatient care. That doesn't mean the eating disorder has been cured, nor does it even mean that your child is out of danger. However, before your child is discharged, you can request a visit from the hospital social worker or discharge planner who may be able to provide eating disorder–related resources for your family.

"It took two weeks before our son was stable enough to be released. And at that point, we thought, this is it. This will fix it. He will realize this is dangerous. He'll straighten up, he'll get past it. He'll get out of the hospital and get back to his old self. We still believed that a few trips to the doctor and some medicine will cure it. And that didn't happen at all. At that point, we started talking to doctors about our next options. We knew that he couldn't keep living like this."

Nonmedical Residential Care

Residential treatment doesn't fix an eating disorder. What it can do is buy time to work on the eating disorder as long as the primary focus is restoration to full nutrition. It can be an appropriate choice if your child is not safe from self-injury, if his medical condition warrants it, or if parents simply do not have the time or ability to supervise refeeding as necessary. However, many counselors agree that if the family isn't going to back that up with a zero-tolerance attitude about disorder eating behaviors on the return home, then it is a waste of time.

When Residential Care Is Appropriate

There are some indications that inpatient care may be the most appropriate next step for your child with an eating disorder:

- The person has been in outpatient care and has not been showing improvement.

- There are complicated family issues to work through.
- The person is self-harming.
- The person cannot control restricting or purging behaviors without strong supervision.
- There are trauma issues that would be too difficult to uncover and deal with in outpatient treatment.
- There is a secondary diagnosis present that would benefit from intensive focused treatment.

Perhaps the biggest indicator for residential care is that a full-time caregiver is not available to supervise the child at home and the child needs such supervision to recover. Most research agrees that family-centered therapy is best, and it can be difficult to fully engage the family and empower them to care for their child if the child is not living at home and in fact may be hours away.

How to Choose Residential Care

If you are considering a residential treatment facility, you may feel a sense of urgency to get your child enrolled immediately. It may feel like a crisis, but it is critical to carefully choose the best treatment center for your child, which may not necessarily be the first one you can find.

Take the time to speak with staff members about the specific costs, including insurance coverage and out-of-pocket expenses. It is important to remember that even if the facility is in your insurance network, there may be out-of-pocket expenses for specific treatments that may not be covered.

"We made the rather naive assumption that once our insurance company approved a fourteen-day stay at the residential center, that the costs would be covered at 90 percent. And they were, mostly. We had to pay for the 10 percent of the bill for the first thirty days, but we weren't prepared for the additional expenses that insurance didn't cover. Certain therapies, like art or music therapy, for example, weren't covered and we were charged $150 an hour per session several times a week. We spent thousands more than we anticipated. We made a big mistake in not asking the right questions," says Bill, whose daughter spent three months in the treatment center.

 Essential

One of the most comprehensive resources for residential eating disorder treatment centers online can be found at *www.edreferral.com*. They provide information on treatment centers, physicians, counselors, and other specialists.

What to Expect from a Residential Treatment Center

Be prepared to give up almost complete control of your child once admitted to a residential treatment center. While such centers are very thorough in their care, you will be permitted to speak to and visit only on very limited occasions and when the center says that you can. There will be a list of rules and regulations, as well as levels of privileges that have to be earned as the child progresses through the program. When rules are broken, there are specific consequences that will follow. You can count on consistency as the hallmark of a residential treatment center. Your child will have set times of the day to get up, take part in assorted activities, eat, and go to bed. The routines, rules, and expectations will be explained to your child upon admission.

 Alert

One risk of an eating disorder treatment center is that the child will be surrounded by people with eating disorders. The potential problem is that they can compete with one another to lose weight, or they can share tips and tricks to lose weight or fool the scale.

Rules and regulations regarding meals are very clear. Your child may or may not have food choices but will be supervised carefully during meals and afterward to make sure no purging occurs. Living in a residential treatment center is not easy, and your child will likely complain. Eating disorder programs will not usually accept children younger than twelve. Many eating disorder programs have a spiritual component, so you may wish to confirm that the center's spiritual orientation is similar to your own if that is important to you.

Outpatient Care Options

Outpatient treatment typically means a scheduled appointment with a medical or mental health professional. Outpatient therapy can consist of talk therapy, visits with a physician or psychiatrist, and other ancillary therapies such as art or music therapy. The needs of your child, and the availability of resources, will direct the frequency of those visits. As with all other treatment, your health insurance company will dictate the number of visits they will pay for. Receiving outpatient care can be an effective part of treatment at any stage of your child's recovery. It may include individual therapy, family therapy, and group therapy, as well as intensive outpatient or partial hospitalization programs.

Group Therapy

Group therapy sessions are led by a trained psychotherapist and may cover everything from healthy eating to coping with the urge to binge. Ideally, group members give and receive advice and support each other. The risk, of course, is that unhealthy people are now in a group of equally unhealthy people. While eating disorders are not contagious, children and young adults can take advantage of the situation by learning new ways to trick the scale or lose weight. A group therapy situation must be led by a seasoned professional who provides clear direction for the group.

Intensive Outpatient Program

Intensive outpatient programs, sometimes called IOPs, are also referred to as partial hospitalization programs (PHPs). Some clinics may have both of these programs and differentiate between them according to the number of hours of programming per week. Some programs will meet multiple days per week for several hours at a time, while others will meet for twelve hours a day five to seven days a week. They usually include a variety of components, including group and individual therapy, and may include at least one meal or snack. The more intensive programs that last all day may have all meals at the treatment facility.

 Essential

You are likely to hear that your child will never completely recover from an eating disorder. If you hear this from an eating disorder professional, then flee. Families Empowered and Supported Treating Eating Disorders describe that philosophy as a disabling and self-perpetuating myth. Find someone who can treat your child who believes in recovery.

No Perfect Answers

There are no perfect answers to finding the right eating disorder treatment for your child. Just as each family and each patient is unique, treatment recommendations for your child are best made collaboratively with experienced experts in the eating disorder field, after a thorough multidisciplinary evaluation, and in close collaboration with psychiatric and medical clinical teams.

CHAPTER 11

Understanding Medication Options

E ating disorders are not simply about emotions; they are a complex neurobiological problem. They are often also accompanied by depression, anxiety, obsessive-compulsive disorder (OCD), and other problems that are often caused by a biochemical imbalance. As such, they can often be improved by medication. There isn't a perfect pill that will cure your child's eating disorder, but there are a number of medications that have proven to be helpful to a number of people with eating disorders.

Why Medication?

There is no cure for eating disorders, nor is there a standard medication that is going to solve your child's eating disorder. Good nutrition is the best medication for an eating disorder, and after that, pharmacological treatment may well help alleviate some of the surrounding problems, such as anxiety or depression. If a child is not eating, however, malnutrition may well impact the efficacy of any medication given. Medication can be a short-term resource that can be discontinued at a later point, but it can help reduce the symptoms of other mental health issues that may get in the way of treatment.

Help from the Medicine Cabinet

When you are looking for a solution to your child's eating disorder, what you long for is something—anything—that will make her better. You may be hesitant to look at medication as a treatment option and are concerned that your child may trade one dependency for another or is using pills as a crutch. Think of it this way: your child's eating disorder is a serious problem that has the potential to cause severe physical harm. If your child had any other disease with the potential to cause harm, whether it was cancer or diabetes, you wouldn't hesitate to use medication.

 Alert

If a friend or other member of your family takes medication for anxiety or depression, it is important not to share that medication with your child to see how she will respond. A child's age, allergies, and symptoms all need to be factored in when writing a prescription.

The Limitations of Medication

Not all patients respond to each medication. Medication alone cannot cure eating disorders, but it can help. Children and adults with eating disorders should also be in some type of therapy in addition to being on medication. Medication can be a valuable tool in your toolbox, but it isn't a perfect solution, nor is it a quick fix. It may take months to find the right combination of medications and dosages. Be patient with the process, and keep a journal recording physical and emotional changes you notice.

Getting Started on Medication

For some eating disorder sufferers and their families, medications have been a blessing. They have helped to bring down the anxiety levels to a point where talk therapy and refeeding can begin and be effective. For others, medications have been a curse. Increased angry outburst, rages, and more severe anxiety have all affected some children and teens prescribed medications for eating disorders. Not everyone will react to the same medication in the same way. The good news is that parents can generally tell if the medication is helpful within a month or so after beginning medication therapy. If the benefits do not outweigh the side effects, then medication can be discontinued and other treatment options can be pursued.

 Essential

Unless a child has an immediate allergic reaction to a medication, it is important not to discontinue the medication without speaking to the prescribing health care provider. Some medications can be abruptly discontinued, while others need to be gradually decreased.

"The medication I wanted doesn't exist," explained Sarah, whose daughter's eating disorder surfaced for the first time at age eleven. "I wanted the medicine that would bring me my daughter back. The fun, sweet, charming daughter who played and laughed and didn't act as though eating dinner was torture. I wanted the daughter back who didn't carve into her legs with a razor blade or cut out pictures of models and glue them into her 'ana' journal. I had to settle for what medication did exist."

A year later, and still on antianxiety medication, Sarah's daughter is doing better. "It didn't cure her eating disorder, but it made coping with her anxiety easier. And now, if she misses a day or two, she can feel the difference and realizes that, at least for right now, it's still helpful for her. The scars are fading and the weight is stable. For us, at least, the medication worked."

Who Is Prescribing the Medication?

Prescribing psychotropic medications is always tricky, and it is especially so with children and teenagers. While your family physician can prescribe medication, a psychiatrist who is knowledgeable about *eating disorders* is an integral part of your child's treatment plan. Ideally, the psychiatrist has experience treating children your age and with an eating disorder.

Trial and Error

When your child begins a new medication, expect a trial period during which the medication is evaluated by both the individual and the medical professional. If the side effects are manageable but the medication does not appear to be working initially, then the dosage may be adjusted. More often than not, a variety of medications may need to be tested before a good fit is found.

"I had this perception about medicine that was completely wrong," explained Joe, whose daughter's eating disorder began at fifteen. "I had this concept that you go to the doctor for X problem, and the doctor prescribes the medication that works on X. That isn't necessarily the way it is for bulimia or other eating disorders. You go in and the doctor says, 'We'll try this and see what happens.' And then you came back in a month and you say 'Nothing changed,' so you get more of the first medication and then another one on top of that one. I walked away from more than one appointment feeling as though my daughter was a guinea pig in some horrible experiment.

"I wish I had known that medications could take months to work, that it often took multiple visits to find the right dose, and, even then, sometimes we just didn't know if she was improving or just being more secretive. I used to hope there was a blood test to use as criteria to see if she was getting better or not."

Many times, medications are transitional and may only be needed a short time. Just because your child is prescribed a particular medication doesn't mean that it will be needed forever. You might have an emotional reaction if your child is prescribed an antianxiety or antipsychotic medication. Do not let the type of medication that has been prescribed become an additional stressor for you or your child.

Evidence-Based Treatment

Over and over again, advocates for eating disorder treatment recommend evidence-based treatment to help decide how to best help your child. Unfortunately, there is not yet enough evidence-based pharmacological treatment for children and teenagers suffering from eating disorders. There are small studies that suggest some medications, such as fluoxetine (*Prozac*), may be helpful both in treating the eating disorder and in preventing relapse. Trying to determine which medications are currently recommended is like trying to shoot a moving target. Your best bet to find accurate information is to do your own research, connect with a few resource organizations (located in Appendix B), and stay up to date on current recommendations.

Medication Types

The type of medication used is dependent on the specific type of eating disorder and how it manifests in your child. For example, an appetite suppressant may be used in someone with a binge disorder, while a young person who is depressed and anorexic may benefit from an antidepressant. Medications may include antidepressants, antianxiety medications, sleeping medications, antipsychotic medications, or others.

Antidepressants

Antidepressants do well in clinical studies for treating anorexia and bulimia. In fact, antidepressants may also decrease binge eating in people with bulimia and may also help people with binge eating disorder. However, studies also show that relapse rates are high when the drug is discontinued, further illustrating the importance of understanding that medication is not a cure for eating disorders. The most popular types of antidepressants are called selective serotonin reuptake inhibitors (SSRIs) and include:

- Fluoxetine (*Prozac*)
- Citalopram (*Celexa*)
- Sertraline (*Zoloft*)
- Paroxetine (*Paxil*)
- Escitalopram (*Lexapro*)

Side Effects

Drowsiness is a common side effect, as is headache and upset stomach. The symptoms will usually subside within a few weeks. One of the potential problems of an antidepressant is that when a person begins taking it, anxiety can increase, at least temporarily. Sometimes antidepressants cause dryness of the mouth. If that happens, your child can use artificial saliva preparations to lubricate the oral tissues, but avoiding carbonated foods or drinks and using sugarless or xylitol-containing candies or mints should help increase salivary flow.

Understanding the Risks

There has been a significant amount of press surrounding antidepressants and teenagers, and it can be frustrating and overwhelming for parents to know what to do if an antidepressant is recommended for their teen. In a nutshell, a comprehensive review of pediatric trials suggested that, for children and adolescents with major depression and anxiety disorders, it is likely that the benefits of antidepressant medications outweigh their potential risks of doing harm.

However, the FDA wanted parents to better understand the risks regarding antidepressants and teenagers and young adults, so they issued a warning that says, despite the relative safety and popularity of SSRIs and other antidepressants, some studies have suggested there may be unintentional effects on patients in this age group. The primary concern is that up to 4 percent of those taking such antidepressants thought about or attempted suicide (although no suicides occurred). This is compared to 2 percent of those who received placebos. This concern generated the "black box warning" that can now be found on all antidepressants. A black box warning is the most serious type of warning currently available on a prescription drug label.

The warning emphasizes that patients of all ages taking antidepressants should be closely monitored, especially when they are in the initial weeks of treatment. Possible adverse reactions to look for include:

- Worsening depression
- Suicidal thinking or behavior
- Any unusual changes in behavior such as sleeplessness, agitation, or withdrawal from normal social situations

The warning also suggests that families and caregivers should be informed of the need for close monitoring and should report any changes to the physician. The latest information from the FDA can be found on their website at *www.fda.gov.*

 Fact

The two treatments that have been documented by evidence-based scientific studies to have the best short-term success rates are cognitive behavioral therapy (CBT) and high-dose fluoxetine.

Antianxiety Medications

Antianxiety medications may be helpful for children and teenagers in the treatment of severe anxiety. There are several types of antianxiety medications, including benzodiazepines, antihistamines, and what is known as atypicals. Examples of benzodiazepines include:

- Alprazolam (*Xanax*)
- Lorazepam (*Ativan*)

- Diazepam (*Valium*)
- Clonazepam (*Klonopin*)

Examples of antihistamines include diphenhydramine (*Benadryl*) and hydroxyzine (*Vistaril*). Examples of antianxiety medications that are atypical include buspirone (*Buspar*) and zolpidem (*Ambien*).

Fluoxetine

Fluoxetine is an antidepressant, but it is one of the most commonly used medications for eating disorders. It is the generic name for a medication that is also sold under the name Prozac and Serafim. Fluoxetine is currently the recommended medication for treating eating disorders. It is also used to treat mental health issues that may occur with an eating disorder, such as depression, obsessive-compulsive disorder (characterized by bothersome thoughts that will not go away and the strongly felt need to perform certain behaviors over and over), as well as panic attacks (sudden and unexpected short periods of extreme fear).

Taking Fluoxetine

This medication is an antidepressant of the selective serotonin reuptake inhibitor (SSRI) class. It can be taken as a liquid or in caplet form. The caplets are extended release, which means they cannot be cut or divided into smaller dosages. Sometimes sleep disturbances occur with fluoxetine, so it is recommended to be taken in the morning with breakfast. The first few doses may cause some gastrointestinal upset or nausea, and taking it with a meal should help alleviate most of the nausea. However, it may be ideal to begin taking the medication on the weekend.

Some common side effects with fluoxetine include:

- Anxiety
- Diarrhea

- Dizziness
- Drowsiness
- Dry mouth
- Flulike symptoms (fever, chills, muscle aches)
- Increased sweating
- Loss of appetite
- Nausea
- Nervousness
- Runny nose
- Sore throat
- Stomach upset
- Trouble sleeping

 Alert

Parents who are concerned about side effects their child is experiencing should contact their health care provider or local emergency department. Side effects can be reported to the FDA at *www.fda.gov/medwatch/* or 1-800-FDA-1088 (1-800-332-1088).

Understanding Tolerance

Fluoxetine is a generally an effective, safe medication for many young people. Initial doses of fluoxetine typically begin at 20 mg per day, but may increase to 40 or even 60 mg. Higher doses than that are possible, but uncommon. When your child has been on a low dose for a period of time, he or she may develop tolerance to the medication, and a higher dose may be needed. As with any other medication, it can lose its helpfulness. Before a physician will take your child off, they will generally raise the dosage to see if that helps. Also, the more times your child goes on and off Prozac, the less likely it is to be helpful.

Warning Signs with Fluoxetine

No medication is without risks, even over-the-counter ones. Fluoxetine is no exception. While some side effects may be uncomfortable, but bearable, there are some adverse affects that indicate fluoxetine must be stopped, including indications of a severe allergic reaction, such as:

- Rash
- Hives
- Itching
- Difficulty breathing
- Tightness in the chest
- Swelling of the mouth, face, lips, or tongue
- Unusual hoarseness

Other adverse effects that indicate a problem include bizarre behavior, black or bloody stools, confusion, chest pain, decreased coordination or concentration, exaggerated reflexes, fainting, fast or irregular heartbeat, or excessive sweating.

Less Commonly Prescribed Medications

Mood stabilizers, sleeping aids, and antipsychotics are all used occasionally in the treatment of eating disorders. They are rarely used as the first medication. In fact, if a heath care provider suggests otherwise, ask to see the research that informs his decision. Remember, the most effective care for a child with eating disorders is that which is evidence based, meaning researchers and clinical studies have found that it works well with a number of children and teenagers with the same condition.

Antipsychotics

Antipsychotic medications are typically used to treat schizophrenia and schizophrenia-related disorders, but they can be given for extreme behavior disorders. Although rarely prescribed for children, sometimes teenagers will be given a prescription for these. Some of the more commonly used typical antipsychotic medications include:

- Chlorpromazine (*Thorazine*)
- Haloperidol (*Haldol*)
- Perphenazine (*Trilafon*)
- Fluphenazine (*Prolixin*)

Newer antipsychotic medications are called "atypical" or second-generation antipsychotics.

 Alert

One atypical antipsychotic, clozapine (*Clozaril*), effectively treats breaks with reality but can sometimes cause a serious problem called agranulocytosis, which means an infection can't be found because of a loss of white blood cells. People who take clozapine must have their white blood cell counts checked every week or so.

Other atypical antipsychotics are rarely prescribed to children but will sometimes be given to adolescents when other medications do not work. They include:

- Risperidone (*Risperdal*)
- Olanzapine (*Zyprexa*)
- Quetiapine (*Seroquel*)
- Ziprasidone (*Geodon*)
- Aripiprazole (*Abilify*)
- Paliperidone (*Invega*)

Sleeping Aids

Sometimes when you take one medication, another may be needed to cope with the side effects. Sleeping aids may be given for children and teens who cannot sleep either in general or because of another medication they may be on. Medications that may be prescribed, usually on a short-term basis only, include:

- Trazodone (*Desyrel*)
- Zolpidem (*Ambien*)
- Zaleplon (*Sonata*)
- Diphenhydramine (*Benadryl*)0

 Fact

If your child or teen can't sleep, but you are hesitant to give a prescription medication, talk to your health care provider about melatonin supplements. Available without a prescription, melatonin has a rapid, mild, sleepiness-inducing effect.

Mood Stabilizers

Mood stabilizers are not the first line of defense for eating disorders. However, if a teenager has been diagnosed with bipolar disorder, a mood stabilizer is usually prescribed. Mood stabilizers may be helpful in treating bipolar disorder, aggressive behavior, impulse control disorders, severe mood symptoms, and mood swings (manic and depressive). Examples include:

- Lithium (lithium carbonate, *Eskalith*)
- Valproic acid (*Depakote, Depakene*)
- Carbamazepine (*Tegretol*)
- Gabapentin (*Neurontin*)
- Lamotrigine (*Lamictal*)
- Topiramate (*Topamax*)
- Oxcarbazepine (*Trileptal*)

Anticonvulsant medications, originally used to control seizures, are also sometimes used as mood stabilizers. Adolescents may be prescribed the mood stabilizer valproic acid (*Depakote*)—also known as divalproex sodium—carbamazepine (*Tegretol*), lamotrigine (*Lamictal*), or oxcarbazepine (*Trileptal*).

Medications for Weight Loss

Appetite suppressants or weight loss aids are rarely prescribed to children but are sometimes offered to adolescents. Some physicians may recommend Xenical, also sold over the counter as Alli, for teens with binge eating disorder. It is a fat absorption inhibitor that works by preventing the body from breaking down and absorbing the fat that is eaten with meals. There is no research to suggest that either appetite suppressants or fat absorption inhibitors will work long term, though they may be appropriate until longer-term therapy goals can be reached. Do not give these products to children under eighteen unless directed by a health care provider.

 Essential

> With a fat absorption inhibitor, unabsorbed fat is eliminated in bowel movements, which may make them appear frothy and they usually float. Prepare your child for any changes in his bowel movements.

When taking a fat absorption inhibitor, lower-fat meals must be eaten (less than 30 percent of the calories in a given meal must come from fat) or the side effects may be unpleasant, including:

- Abdominal cramping
- Passing gas
- Leakage of oily stool
- Increased number of bowel movements
- Inability to control bowel movement

The diabetes drug metformin, also known as Glucophage, can also help obese teenagers lose weight even if they don't have the disease. FDA approval is pending, so it is currently an off-label use of the drug, which can cause similar side affects as a fat absorption inhibitor. Early research suggests modest weight loss as long as the person stays on the drug, though weight tends to return within a few months after stopping the medication. However, it is an inexpensive medication and may be effective in helping your child get a jump start on managing their weight.

When You Get a New Prescription

When a physician or psychologist hands a prescription to a parent, a typical response of the parent is to silently take the prescription and get it filled without asking any questions. After all, the doctor knows best. Not anymore. This prescriber may know medications better than the average parent, but as the parent, you are the expert on your child. As such, that means you have an additional responsibility to become actively involved in all aspects of your child's care, including understanding why a prescription was ordered, what the benefits and risks are, and what the expected outcomes should be.

Ask Your Physician

Here are some questions you might want to ask your physician about any new medications:

- Why is my child taking this medication?
- What are the long-term and short-term risks of taking this medication?
- What are the side effects?
- Are there any tests my child will need while taking this medication?

- Is this medication tested on children who have this diagnosis?
- When will this medication begin working?
- How do I know if it is working?
- Is there anything else I should know about this medication?

Ask Your Pharmacist

The best way to prevent medication errors is to arm yourself with as much information as possible. Your local pharmacist can provide a wealth of information on your child's medications and at no additional fee. Make sure you get all of your child's medications at the same pharmacy. Ideally, if the record systems are computerized, an automatic warning should alert the pharmacist if the medication should not be taken due to allergies or other medications your child is taking. Keep a list of all medications your child is taking, including vitamins and over-the-counter pain or cold medicines, and provide copies to health care providers and the pharmacy.

Here are some questions you might want to ask your pharmacist about any new medications prescribed for your child:

- Is there a generic version of this medication?
- What is the correct dosage my child needs to take?
- How often does my child take this medication and when?
- Does my child take this with food?
- What do I do if my child experiences side effects?
- How do I know if my child should stop taking this medicine due to side effects or an allergy?
- Can my child continue taking his or her other medications with it?
- Is there anything else I should know about this medication?

Where to Find Information

Carefully read the prescription insert provided with your child's medication. If such information was not provided, ask the pharmacist for it. The label typically provides basic information, such as the drug name, the dosage, and the frequency. The National Library of Medicine *Drug Information Portal* offers users free information on selected drugs. You can search by category or by drug name. Go to *http://druginfo.nlm.nih.gov/drugportal/drugportal.jsp.*

Giving Your Child Medications

Once you have read and understood the medication instructions, make sure you stick to a regular medication schedule. Medications are designed to work under specific conditions, and if you don't follow medication instructions, the medication may not work or your child may suffer unnecessary side effects. For example, if a medication should be eaten with food, not doing so may result in nausea.

Do not crush your medication and hide it in food or drink without talking to your pharmacist first. If your child is taking an extended-release medication (often identified as such with an XR in the name), then you cannot crush the medication. Plus, if you crush a tablet and mix it in applesauce, for example, then your child may not eat the entire serving and will end up underdosed with no real way of knowing how much she had.

Making Medication Decisions

No medications are risk-free; even Tylenol and aspirin have side effects and risks. Doctors must weigh the risks of the treatment compared to the risks of the illness, and parents must do the same. As a parent, you have the right to decide not to give a certain medication to your child. However, if you decide not to give your child a certain medication, it is in your child's best interests to tell the physician why you do not want to put your child on a certain medication. Too often, parents will just accept the prescription and leave, never intending to get the prescription filled.

Weighing the Costs

Depending on your health insurance, where you live, and what pharmacy options you have, the prescribed medication may be prohibitively expensive. If a medication is prescribed for your child, ask if there is a generic version, which is usually significantly less expensive. Understanding your prescription medication coverage and sharing it with your health team will help prescribers be as cost-effective as possible. After all, the best medication in the world won't help if you can't afford to buy it.

Some insurance companies will offer savings if a three-month supply is purchased. Review your health insurance packet or speak with your benefits representative to uncover any medication guidelines and saving opportunities. Chain drugstores often offer savings benefits by becoming a preferred member, and Wal-Mart and Sam's Club offer a list of dozens of medications that can be purchased for $4 to $10.

When to Stop Taking a Medication

Medications should be taken until both the individual and medical professional agree that it is time to stop. If you have concerns about the side effects of a medication, do not just stop taking the medication. There may be problems if you stop a drug immediately.

Medication Noncompliance

As shocking as it may seem, your once obedient and pleasant child may now go out of his way to avoid taking medication, hide it, or even throw it up. Remember, your child has come to depend on his eating disorder as a companion, even though it's a widely dysfunctional and hurtful one. Your child may often perceive medication as another attempt by you to take away something that he depends on. You cannot therefore assume that your child is going to willingly take his medicine on schedule.

You might also want to be prepared for your teenager to complain mightily about the side effects of the medication and very dramatically plead to be taken off of it, especially if it is a medication that increases the appetite. In fact, in one study on epilepsy medicine, over one-fourth of parents reported noncompliance with medication for their children because of the side effects. Either medication is an appropriate treatment or it isn't for your child. Taking medication irregularly or not at all doesn't help anyone, not your child or the treatment team.

Eagle Eye

"Katy, go upstairs and take your morning meds, please," yells Katy's mom from downstairs. She's seventeen, after all, how hard is it to open the pillbox and take out the precounted, presorted pills? It depends on your child, on the medication, on your child's current frame of mind, and maybe even the order of the planets. A child with an eating disorder can be amazingly manipulative and is often willing to lie to achieve the desired goal of the eating disorder.

While you may not have realized it, you may well turn into one of those nurses in the movies who gives the medication and asks the patient to open her mouth. That means you need to take full responsibility for the medications. If you decide to follow the medication therapy that your physician has recommended, then you need to keep the medications away from your child and any other children in the household, maintain a regular dosing schedule, and make sure that when you give the medication that your child actually puts the medication in her mouth and swallows it.

After you give the medication, it is wise to have the child stay with you for a few minutes. If she has placed the pill under the tongue or in the pouch of the cheek, it will be difficult to carry on a conversation. If your child is prone to bulimia, then you will want to keep a close eye on her for at least half an hour. Of course, that means you will need to encourage your child to use the restroom before taking the medication, as nothing makes a child have to go to the bathroom as being told she cannot go.

Do Not Waver

"My daughter would beg me not to have the newest medication her doctor would prescribe. She hated it. She hated the way it made her feel. She would cry and look so convincing there were times I considered not making her take it until I had the chance to call the doctor and talk to him about the possibility of switching. Actually, I did more than consider it, I let her stop. More than once, even. She was just so convincing and pitiful and I felt so bad for her," explains Sandra, mother of Alexandria, a fifteen-year-old girl with anorexia.

"I was embarrassed, but I 'fessed up to her doctor. Her doctor asked me what I would do if she had cancer and she was prescribed chemotherapy. Would I let her manipulate her way out of taking it then? It was a silly question; of course I wouldn't. Her life would be at stake. Her doctor let that answer sit in the air for a while before I got it. There's no more playing around with medication at our house. If my daughter wanted to have a discussion about it, I have her keep a symptom diary and be prepared to state her case to her physician at her next appointment. That way she still has some input into the decisions we make about her health care and she feels as though she is being heard, but she isn't manipulating me anymore."

CHAPTER 12

Understanding Counseling

There are three basic pieces to eating disorder recovery: full nutrition, family support, and effective counseling that addresses the disordered thinking related to disordered eating. If any of these three pieces are missing, then full recovery can be delayed. The danger in postponing full recovery is that the longer the disease continues, the more difficult it is to cure. Effective counseling is a critical part of your child's full recovery from the eating disorder.

Why Counseling Is Necessary

If an eating disorder is a disease based on genetics, then why is counseling important? Perhaps one day there will be an eating disorder pill that will instantly cure someone once an eating disorder begins. Until then, counseling is necessary because the disease affects the way the person thinks. The way your child thinks affects the way your child feels. The way your child feels affects the way your child acts. For example, your child thinks, "I look fat in this bathing suit." She then feels frustrated, angry, and scared. She acts on those feelings by refusing to eat her next meal, by cutting herself, or by feeling so bad about herself that she binges, then, in a fit of guilt and shame, she purges. A healthy person can look in the mirror and think, "I don't look perfect in this bathing suit, but

I look pretty good" or "I don't look the way I would like to in this bathing suit; I should probably get back to exercising a couple of times a week." Counseling can change the way your child thinks, feels, and acts.

Compliance Isn't Necessary

Your child doesn't have to want to go into counseling for it to be effective. After all, your child doesn't necessarily believe that he has a problem. No problem, no need for a solution—it's that simple. And you may hear people tell you that counseling is not going to work unless your child is ready to do the work. A good counselor doing the right kind of counseling can be effective, even when your child doesn't want to go and actively resists treatment. Remember, counseling cannot be fully effective unless full nutrition is underway. Malnutrition can affect your child's thinking for months, and healing the mind requires the body to be healing as well.

Understanding Recovery Resistance

Who wouldn't want to get better and heal from an eating disorder? It can be hard for family and friends to understand why a child with an eating disorder isn't likely to comply with therapy. To explain why, Dan Reiff, MPH RD, coauthor of *Eating Disorders: Nutrition Therapy in the Recovery Process*, uses an analogy that he calls "The Helicopter Story." He suggests thinking of the person who is considering eating disorder recovery to a person who is unable to swim and who has been stranded in the middle of the ocean with only a life jacket to keep her afloat.

The stranded person knows that if she is not rescued by the helicopter, then she will likely drown or die of hypothermia. The problem is that the helicopter team tells the swimmer that she must give up her life jacket in order for her to be pulled on board. It feels terrifying, and it's also the reason, says Reiff, why people with eating disorders need time and lots of expert support in order to give up their behaviors and recover completely.

Fact

Counselors will often ask people with an eating disorder to write a letter to the eating disorder thanking them for what it does for them and then listing all of the reasons why he or she doesn't want to give up the eating disorder. While it may be painful to hear, sometimes such a list can help parents understand their child's reluctance to let go of an eating disorder.

Think of it this way: you go to your doctor for your annual checkup. The doctor walks in the room holding a medication you have never seen before. You ask what it is and she responds that it is time for your chemotherapy. She goes on to explain that the chemotherapy is very toxic, that it has horrific side effects, including extreme nausea, vomiting, diarrhea, and a painful rash all over your body. You will lose your hair and be in too much pain to sleep or work, but it will cure the cancer. You explain that there has been a serious mistake—you do not have cancer. You haven't had any tests done, nor are there strange masses or symptoms of anything. You feel healthy as a horse; the doctor has clearly made a mistake, and you do everything in your power to explain to the physician that she is wrong. As strongly as you would fight against taking that chemotherapy, that's what "normal" eating feels like to a person with an eating disorder. To stop purging or binging or restricting feels as dangerous as it would be to take that medication. And for most people with an eating disorder, they are convinced they aren't sick, so medication isn't even necessary.

Where to Begin

Finding a counselor who competently treats eating disorders can be like finding a needle in a haystack. In her book, *Eating with Your Anorexic*, Laura Collins describes the search for a treatment team member as going to an oncologist for a brain tumor and having the oncologist respond by asking if you could have something easier to treat like breast cancer. After all, brain cancer is messy and hard and breast cancer is a lot better to work with. Depression and anxiety? You can have a line of counselors knee-deep for those kinds of issues. It can be much more difficult to locate a counselor who knows how to treat eating disorders from a family-centered approach and sees eating disorders as a disease and not as a result of a stubborn child or dysfunctional family.

Counseling Approaches

The first step in finding an appropriate counselor is knowing what you are looking for. It can be tempting to embrace the first counselor you can find who has an opening and is willing to treat your child, but don't. Not all counselors work with children with eating disorders, and not all counselors who work with eating disorders use an approach that is most effective in treating eating disorders. Even if a counselor says he is an expert in eating disorder treatment, you will need to know what type of therapy the counselor uses.

There are several types of therapies, and not all of them are effective in treating eating disorders. In fact, there are over 400 specific types of therapies, although most fit into one of a handful of schools, each of which has its own theories and techniques. Some therapies are a blend of several approaches. You'll need to understand a broad overview to see what type of therapy will work for your child.

- **Psychoanalysis**, based on the work of Sigmund Freud, is the most long-lasting form of talk therapy (it can take years) and is perhaps the most widely known approach.
- **Psychodynamic** is talk therapy on a smaller scale, while still focusing on the unconscious, personal development, and the relationship between therapist and patient.

- **Cognitive therapies** focus on negative thoughts and learning to replace irrational thoughts with rational ones.
- **Behavioral therapy** is often paired with cognitive therapies and focuses on changing unwanted behavior, especially related to anxiety-inducing situations.
- **Interpersonal psychotherapy** focuses on resolving relational conflicts, improving communication, and building a more solid support network.
- **Experiential therapy** focuses on learning to tell the difference between healthy and unhealthy emotional responses but places a stronger emphasis on developing a supportive and empathetic relationship between the therapist and the patient.

Choosing Evidence-Based Counseling

Now that you know there are so many different types of counseling to choose from, which one do you choose? Parents of children with eating disorders must make an informed decision that is right for their own child. One way to make that decision is to look for counseling approaches that have been studied in research projects. What does the evidence say about this particular kind of therapy for this particular kind of problem? You might well have a close friend who loved her therapist, but if that counselor doesn't have experience with eating disorders, or worse, uses an approach that keeps the child obsessing, then the counselor may do more harm. To date, the research indicates that cognitive behavioral therapy with strong family leadership and involvement is the most effective and efficient way of treating children and adults with multiple types of disordered eating.

Even if your child is in a residential treatment program or intensive outpatient program, ask about the kind of therapy used. Do not waste valuable time, energy, and resources on counseling approaches that have not yet been proven to be effective. Eating disorder research is still in its infancy. In time, other psychological approaches may prove to be as effective, or even more so, than cognitive behavioral approaches. That is why staying abreast of the current research is so critical.

Cognitive Behavioral Therapy

Some counselors use cognitive behavioral therapy (CBT). Cognitive behavioral therapy is a form of counseling that focuses on changing the dysfunctional thoughts and behaviors involved in disordered eating. The benefit of CBT, practitioners believe, is that once you learn to change your thinking, you can then change your feelings, and your actions. Cognitive behavioral therapy for eating disorders also usually involves nutrition education, a safety plan for when feelings are out of control, and relaxation techniques.

Cognitive behavioral therapy (CBT) has been proven to be more effective than antidepressant medications alone in reducing the average number of binge eating episodes. However, for most types of eating disorders, both an antidepressant and CBT combined are the most effective.

 Essential

A new evidence report by ECRI Institute comparing the effectiveness of various treatments for bulimia nervosa indicates that cognitive behavioral therapy is more effective than antidepressant medications and supportive therapies in improving eating disorder symptoms.

Dialectical Behavior Therapy

Dialectical behavior therapy (DBT) is an offshoot of cognitive behavioral therapy. There is slightly more emphasis on feelings, but research indicates that dialectical behavioral therapy may be ideal for eating disorder patients who have co-occurring conditions like depression. The emphasis in dialectical behavioral therapy is often on teaching disordered eating patients to accept themselves, and unhealthy attitudes in regards to eating, shape, and weight may also be addressed. Dialectical behavior therapy often includes both weekly group therapy sessions as well as individual treatment sessions. Topics covered often include:

- Skills in distress tolerance
- Mindfulness
- Emotional regulation
- Interpersonal effectiveness

Family Involvement

Family therapy, also known as family behavioral therapy, is not as daunting as it sounds. Nor is it an opportunity to sit in a room while a counselor points fingers and accuses the parents of creating the eating disorder. Family therapy can be an effective tool if it is used in conjunction with other support tools.

What the Research Says

Research indicates again and again that one of the single most important factors in a child's improvement is the involvement of the family. In a research study with eighty bulimic teens, half of the teenagers went through traditional psychotherapy, and the others were placed in psychotherapy and family therapy. Months later, the success rate for those in the family therapy was more than double that of those in psychotherapy alone. In fact, almost all of those who were in family therapy had stopped disordered eating behaviors, compared to just 18 percent of those in psychotherapy. One of the best reasons family involvement is so critical? Kids stay involved in therapy longer when Mom and Dad are invested. In family-based therapy, about 15 percent of families will quit early, while non-family-based therapy has a dropout rate of nearly 50 percent. When families are actively involved in treatment, children are less likely to die, treatment takes less time, and both parents and children rate it more favorably than child-focused treatment alone.

Healthy Family Involvement

In a family-based model, eating disorder patients are treated not only as individuals but as members of a family unit. The assumption should also be made that parents will be active and involved team members who are both positive and necessary. The parents of the patient may also need appropriate education, coaching, and support, even though they are the experts on their own child. Some sessions with the counselor should involve the entire family, and you should be informed about and feel comfortable with the goals and methods used in the counseling sessions.

The Perfect Fit

Sometimes the counselor is not going to be the perfect fit. He may be a good-enough fit. Your ability to locate a counselor in your area that does the right kind of counseling and has some experience with eating disorders may be a Herculean task. Cities that have pediatric hospitals attached to their medical schools often have effective programs, or at least dietitians or physicians who can offer referral suggestions. If that's not an option, talk with your pediatrician or primary care provider.

 Essential

Not sure where to begin looking for an eating disorder treatment professional? Start with the Association for Eating Disorder Professionals, a global professional association committed to leadership in eating disorders research, education, treatment, and prevention (*www.aedweb.org*).

Teachable Moments

In some cases, a counselor may use cognitive behavioral therapy but may not have much experience in working with children or even with eating disorders. What to do? If this counselor is open to learning, receptive to resources and even suggestions from you, and you are limited by resources or geography in finding a better fit, then go with the counselor who is willing to learn and walk alongside of you. F.E.A.S.T. (Families Empowered and Supporting Treatment of Eating Disorders) offers information for treatment professionals on best practices in eating disorder treatment specifically related to the Maudsley method, the highly successful family-based treatment approach where parents play an active role in refeeding their child with the goal of restoring weight to a range that is appropriate for their age, height, and optimal medical and psychiatric functioning.

Geographical Limitations

Not everyone has access to appropriately trained eating disorder professionals. What can a parent do? In some cases, distance care may be appropriate. In other words, your child may be able to participate in a counseling session via Skype or telephone. It isn't ideal, but it is better than having no therapeutic support or having a counselor who doesn't share the same treatment goals. Keep in mind that a therapist thousands of miles away may be poorly equipped to help you in an emergency.

 Essential

Organizations such as the International Society for Mental Health Online and the newly formed Online Therapy Institute now provide the means to verify that counselors who practice online are verified and reputable.

"What worked for us was traveling to Oregon to a well-respected treatment center. We spent a week there for a rather intensive physical and psychological assessment and started family sessions and some personal sessions with our daughter. We then did follow-up work remotely. Once my daughter had developed an initial rapport with the counselor and we had the opportunity to meet face-to-face, we all felt comfortable continuing with the process via Skype. It isn't what I would have chosen if I had better alternatives. But the counselors near us were just not fit to treat an eating disorder. This was a less-than-perfect solution that was still the best option we had, and I'm grateful for it," explains Jon, a dad of a daughter with bulimia.

 Fact

While telemedicine or teletherapy may be helpful, your health insurance hasn't quite caught up. Most families will need to pay out of pocket for these sessions.

What Matters Most

Getting your child healthy and keeping your child safe is your primary responsibility. Other people may have a vested interest in your child's well-being, but not the way you do. That means you will likely have people in your life who will tell you they disagree with the decisions you are making for your child. Decide before it happens that you can appreciate the concern the person is offering, and simply offer to provide information on the latest eating disorder research if they are interested in learning more. You will encounter more than one professional with the appropriately impressive number of letters after their name who will say the most asinine, untrue statements about eating disorders. Expect it to happen.

"It was my daughter's second hospitalization and we had our first family meeting. I was feeling so hopeful about this place because they were affiliated with a local children's hospital and they seemed to say all the right things. The counselor met with my daughter and then during the family session, the counselor explained, in front of my seventeen-year-old daughter, how the birth of our second child a decade earlier had caused a psychic crisis that precipitated the drop in self-esteem, and hence, the eating disorder. My jaw almost literally dropped as she explained how we caused the eating disorder by not showering her with more affection when her sister was born. That was the last time that counselor had the privilege of having my family's attention," said Sarah, who did find a therapist who understood disordered eating.

 Fact

Be prepared when someone either offers unwanted advice or asks what he or she can do to help. Send them to *www.feast-ed.org/ TheFacts/Howotherscanhelp.aspx*, an article on how others can help, prepared by the nonprofit group F.E.A.S.T. (Families Empowered and Supporting Treatment of Eating Disorders). Encourage others to do some extra reading while they are there.

You're Fired

At any point, you can fire your therapist. The counselor doesn't have to like you. The world won't end if you have to change counselors, or even if the counselor is angry that you stop bringing your child. If you feel as though the information your child is receiving isn't accurate, or if the counselor is attempting to minimize the seriousness of the situation, blame you or family dynamics for the disorder, or is assisting your child in negotiating regarding full nutrition or other behaviors, you must end therapy immediately.

Safety First

Safety must always come first, even above daily nutrition. Of course, without daily full nutrition, any mental symptoms are more likely to continue. A child's potential to commit suicide must be assessed throughout the life of the eating disorder. Research suggests that suicide is one of the primary causes of premature death in patients with eating disorders. The suicide mortality rate is twenty-three times higher among bulimics and anorexics than that of the general population. That statistic places the suicide rate among disordered eating patients among the highest in all psychiatric disorders.

Your child is at an increased risk for suicide with these additional factors:

- Alcohol abuse, including any use by anyone under the legal drinking age
- Mood disorder
- Presence of anxiety
- Drug use
- High sense of spiritual acceptance
- Perfectionism
- ED severity (greater the severity, the higher the risk)
- Poor decision-making skills
- History of self-harm
- People who binge/purge or who have EDNOS are at highest risk

If your child has one or more risk factors in addition to the eating disorder or if you are just concerned about the potential for self-harm, discuss your concerns with your treatment team, especially your mental health professional.

 **Essential**

You might have a list of emergency numbers by your phone, such as poison control or the pediatrician's on-call number. Add these twenty-four-hour crisis lines with trained volunteers and professional counselors in case your child ever needs them: Bulimia and Self-Help Hotline: 1-314-588-1683, National Suicide Hotline: 800-SUICIDE (800-784-2433).

If your child is actively threatening suicide, or is talking about suicide and has a plan, then waiting for the next counseling appointment is not an appropriate action. If your child is willing to go, or you are able to get him in the car (always with another adult for support), then take your child to the nearest hospital. If your child is so unstable that you do not think you can safely transport him to the hospital, then call 911 so an ambulance can provide the transportation.

CHAPTER 13

Complementary Therapies

Complementary therapies for eating disorders are a diverse range of health-related treatments that are not part of mainstream or traditional medical care. Generally speaking, complementary therapies like yoga, meditation, and art and music therapy are thought to increase well-being, aid relaxation, and promote good mental health. Many parents find that using complementary therapies can be a helpful addition for their child's eating disorder treatment.

What Is Complementary Care?

Complementary therapies like spiritual practices or art and music therapy typically involve a more holistic approach to treating people, which means to treat the whole person and consider physical, psychological, and spiritual needs rather than focusing on the symptoms of the illness. Complementary therapies are sometimes called alternative treatments. Complementary therapies may be a better term because *complementary* suggests that these treatments can be beneficial to people when used in addition to medical treatment. They may also be referred to as natural, nonconventional, holistic, or even complementary medicine.

Why Complementary Approaches

Complementary approaches to treating eating disorders can be useful because they may provide help in a number of ways. Many people with eating disorders suggest that complementary therapies find it helpful, for example, to practice mindfulness and living in the moment. Treatment options may be helpful in decreasing eating disorder symptoms, food preoccupation, as well as relieve anxiety and depression symptoms. However, complementary approaches are exactly that—they are meant to complement the medical treatment your child is receiving and not replace them.

What to Consider

There are dozens of different complementary therapies to consider. While most complementary therapies are completely safe and have little potential to do harm, there are always some risks in treatment. Be particularly wary of those that involve herbal remedies or nutritional supplements or therapies because they may interact with prescription medication.

If you are considering such options, here are a few key reminders:

- Choose a qualified practitioner
- Ask about the practitioner's qualification and experience
- Inform all professionals involved in your child's care about all your treatments and medications
- Find a reliable source for your information about therapies
- Don't take remedies from an unreliable source; this includes the Internet

 Essential

Do not be misled by anyone who promises a cure for your child's eating disorder. No reputable professional of any kind would claim to be able to cure an eating disorder.

Complementary Care Expenses

One of the concerns that arises when considering complementary care is the expense involved. Most complementary therapists operate independently, and fees can be high, especially for one-on-one care. It is rare that health insurance will cover the cost of such programs, although if residential care is covered, then such programs may be included in the cost of the program fees. For those living in a larger metropolitan area, group programs may be available, which are typically offered at a lowered cost.

 Essential

One caveat to group work is that sometimes a group of people with eating disorders aren't always good companions for each other. Young people with eating disorders can not only inwardly compete with one another, but they may also share unhealthy tips like how to "fool" a scale.

Animal-Assisted Therapy

Animal-assisted therapy is defined as the use of animals to facilitate positive changes in a broad spectrum of therapeutic settings, and to promote physical, emotional, cognitive, and social improvement for people with special needs. A number of residential treatment centers use animal-assisted therapy, though you may be able to find additional ways to incorporate animals into your child's recovery. Some counselors may incorporate socialized dogs and cats, among other animals, to provide a very soothing, calming, and nonjudgmental presence in a therapy room. A warm, responsive companion can help patients in a therapy setting feel safe and more capable of engaging in difficult work.

Pet Rescue and Rehabilitation

Animals who are strays or who have been abandoned need a great deal of care, careful attention, and socialization before they can become adopted. When a young person becomes responsible for the rehabilitation of a hurt or discarded animal, it allows him or her to become engaged in meaningful activity and can increase feelings of self-confidence, self-determination, and purpose.

Equine Therapy

For years, horses have been used to help children and adults with special needs and physical rehabilitation. In recent years, their benefits have become widely accepted in relationship to eating disorder patients. There are two critical components in equine therapy, learning horsemanship skills such as grooming, feeding, and saddling, but also developing psychosocial skills while having positive interactions with the horses. Research indicates that equine therapy can aid in developing self-acceptance, self-confidence, communication skills, nurturing abilities, and the ability to be in the moment.

Art Therapy

Art therapy provides an opportunity to address feelings and concerns with a professional art therapist through drawing, painting, or working with clay or other materials in a semi-directed way. Art therapists offer a safe, nonthreatening space in which to explore a variety of feelings that may be difficult to express in other ways. The medical community has become gradually more aware of the positive impact of creative therapies on both the psychological and physical well-being of patients, and as such, art therapy programs are being implemented in many medical settings, including many eating disorder treatment centers.

Art therapists work with clients who have eating disorders using the healing powers inherent in forms of creative expression. Art can be a particularly effective tool and creates an opportunity for a young person to engage in nonverbal forms of communication. By drawing and visually expressing their feelings, even if they can't identify or label their emotions, clients have a starting point from which they can address their issues.

Why It Works

"I agreed to go to art therapy because I didn't want to talk about my feelings. I was exhausted. I have had enough of everyone asking me lots of questions that I didn't even know the answers to. In art therapy, I could use paints and clay to make different things and it helped me see how I felt about different things," said Anna, who worked with a local art therapist for several months. Drawing and creating art can help relieve stress in several ways, by creating distraction, as an outlet for painful emotions, and as an opportunity for a counselor or parent to better understand the artist's pain.

 Fact

Young women who have an eating disorder draw self-portraits with prominently different characteristics than women who do not have an eating disorder. Young women with anorexia are more likely to draw themselves without breasts, with less defined body lines, and smaller figures relative to the page size.

Adding Art Therapy

Children do not have to be "good" in art to participate in art therapy. To find an art therapist near you, contact the official site of the American Art Therapy Association at *www.arttherapy.org*. Some group experiences may be offered or you may be able to get a lower fee by working with an art therapist in training. If you do not have an art therapist in your area, consider getting *The Slender Trap*, a self-discovery food and body workbook for girls and women with all types of eating disorders, by Lauren Stern. Stern is an expert art psychotherapist and licensed professional counselor who has specialized in eating disorders for over twenty-five years. The workbook is easy to read and is filled with creative, thought-provoking exercises. It offers insight into what your daughter is thinking, feeling, and going through as she works to recover from her eating disorder.

Biofeedback

Biofeedback, also known as neurofeedback, involves the science of reconditioning and retraining brain wave patterns. Specifically, the technique uses monitoring instruments in becoming aware of various physiological functions. In other words, patients are trained to improve their health by using signals from their own bodies, especially in regards to anxiety.

How It Works

During a biofeedback session, electrodes are attached to the person's skin. The electrodes then send information to a small monitoring box that then translates the information into a variable tone or visual meter. Using that information, the biofeedback therapist can then lead the patient through a series of helpful mental exercises. Through trial and error, patients can then learn to identify specific mental activities that can bring about the desired physical changes.

How to Incorporate Biofeedback

Biofeedback has been widely practiced since the 1980s. Many different types of practitioners use biofeedback, including neurologists, psychiatrists, psychologists, and counselors. While parents won't be using electrodes and electrical monitoring boxes in their own homes, patients can easily transfer what they learn during those sessions. Some residential treatment centers also offer biofeedback.

 **Essential**

To find a biofeedback practitioner, contact the Association for Applied Psychophysiology and Biofeedback at 1-800-477-8892 / 303-422-8436, or *www.aapb.org.*

Energy Healing

Energy healing is a term for any type of healing that is designed to restore and balance the flow of energy in the body. It is not widely used in clinical settings, but many people have found it to be helpful. According to the American Hospital Association, in 2007, over 800 hospitals in the United States offered reiki, a form of energy healing, as part of hospital services, and the number continues to grow. The Hartford Hospital in Hartford, Connecticut, completed research that suggested that for its patients, reiki improved patient sleep by 86 percent, reduced pain by 78 percent, reduced nausea by 80 percent, and reduced anxiety during pregnancy by 94 percent.

How Energy Healing Works

There is some clinical evidence that this type of energy healing can have a positive effect on people who have mild to moderate mental health problems like depression and anxiety. Energy healers believe that, in addition to a physical body, there is also an energy body made up of individual chakras responsible for different aspects of a person's emotional and physical well-being. With an emotional or physical disharmony, those chakras become unbalanced or blocked. The energy field practitioner acts as a channel of the universal healing energy and harnesses it to unblock and balance the chakras. Practically speaking, they do so by placing their hands at certain positions above the body at certain positions.

How to Incorporate Energy Healing

While many people report a strong sense of relaxation during the treatment as well as a feeling of well-being after treatment, it doesn't have a strong research base, particularly with regards to eating disorders. That being said, engaging in energy healing may be right for some families or for some young people who are open to a more holistic approach. It may help those with eating disorders better connect with their bodies.

 Essential

To find a reiki practitioner near you, check out the International Association of Reiki Professionals (IARP) at *www.iarp.org*.

Herbal Medication

Herbal medication is the use of plant extracts as a means of treating medical problems, whether physical or emotional. While you may not know of many herbal treatments, most people are familiar with one of the most well-known, St. John's Wort (*Hypericum perforatum*). Research has shown powerful evidence that St. John's Wort is as effective as antidepressants when treating mild to moderately severe depression. Another advantage—St. John's Wort has fewer side effects. There are additional herbal medicines like valerian and kava extract that have preliminary research indicating usefulness for treating anxiety. The problem? No research indicates that herbal medications are effective in treating eating disorders.

How to Use Herbal Medications

As another option in using herbal remedies, there are a number of herbs that have been proven to promote the appetite. Herbs from this list may be boiled into a tea and given before meals. They include:

- Peppermint
- Dandelion
- Alfalfa
- Fennel
- Chamomile
- Fenugreek
- Lemon balm

What to Know about Herbal Medications

If you are interested in trying any herbal medication for your child, even in teas, discuss it with your health care provider. While medications like fluoxetine (*Prozac*) have been clinically proven to be effective in treating eating disorders, not everyone can tolerate the side effects of prescription medications, nor is every family is willing to use prescription medication. It is not safe to use herbal medications on a child or adult without speaking with a health care provider, even if those medications can be purchased over the counter at a local drugstore.

 Fact

In ayurveda, an Indian medicine, a bhringaraj oil massage is thought to help relaxation and promote sleep. Massage the scalp and soles of your child's feet with bhringaraj oil before bedtime.

Hypnotherapy

Hypnotherapy is often thought of as the stuff of bad magic shows or people on stage being forced to act like a farm animal. In actuality, hypnotism uses exercises that bring about deep relaxation and an altered state of consciousness, which is also known as a trance. Hypnotherapy is an accepted medical practice that has been proven to relieve a wide range of psychological and physical symptoms. For example, it can help a person reprogram negative thoughts and emotions.

How It Works

Being hypnotized does not involve becoming unconscious or being put to sleep. Someone who is hypnotized continues to have the ability to hear and think. Once they are in the very relaxed state of consciousness, then they are more open to hearing new ways of thinking. There are several stages of hypnosis:

1. Reframe the problem
2. Become relaxed, then engage deeply in the words or images presented by a trained hypnotherapist
3. Dissociate or cultivate the ability to let go of critical thoughts
4. Respond by complying with the hypnotherapist's suggestions
5. Return to usual daytime awareness
6. Reflect on the experience

 Fact

To find a hypnotist who works with people with eating disorders, go to the ED Referral site at *www.edreferral.com*. The referral information is supplied by the providers and is not checked or warranted by EDReferral.com, but the providers have indicated an interest in working with eating disorder patients.

How to Incorporate Hypnotism

Research indicates that hypnotism, also sometimes referred to as guided imagery, can improve the ability of people with eating disorders to self-soothe. Two studies at Mount Sinai Hospital in Toronto found that after six weeks of guided imagery, treatment was extremely successful, with a 70 percent reduction in binging and purging episodes in their patients. In addition, those who participated in guided imagery therapy also showed improvement in attitudes regarding eating, dieting, and body weight.

Meditation

Meditation may help a broad range of individuals to cope with their clinical and nonclinical problems. While there are different types of meditation, most types have in common the practice of sitting quietly and focusing your mind on either an object, your breathing, or a mantra, which is a repeated phrase. As thoughts arise, the person is encouraged to gently acknowledge them without judgment and then let those thoughts drift away while the attention can then be returned to the breath or object. Peter Strong, PhD, a Buddhist psychotherapist and author of *The Path of Mindfulness Meditation*, explains that eating disorder treatment should always involve your physician, but it is also essential to work on changing the underlying emotional drives that compel people to either overindulge or to have extreme food aversion.

Why It Works

There are many studies that indicate that mindfulness meditation techniques can reduce stress and increase personal well-being. Steve Tromans, a hypnotherapist, describes bulimia as a TV show in the mind, one that the sufferer endlessly stars in and that repeats over and over again. "The cure for bulimia, it seems to me, very much lies in learning how to become the 'director' of the show. Meditation can be an excellent route to gaining charge of your day-to-day thoughts. It is very much a training issue, one way or another. The clearer you become in your mind about where you are going, the easier it is to get there."

How to Incorporate Meditation

Over time, meditation practitioners say they can learn to quiet a busy and stressful mind as well as gain a stronger connection to the present moment without the intrusion of any unwanted thoughts. This practice is known as mindfulness or mindfulness meditation and can be practiced at home on your own or in a group. Meditation is often practiced in residential treatment centers. There are many books and online sites that provide information on meditation, though it is best done in a therapeutic setting to help direct the specific thoughts.

Music Therapy

The American Music Therapy Association defines music therapy as the "clinical and evidence-based use of music interventions to accomplish individualized goals within a therapeutic relationship by a credentialed professional who has completed an approved music therapy program." Music therapy techniques may include song writing, singing, drumming, and lyric analysis discussion, among others.

How It Works

Music therapy has been proven to influence mental state, regulate mood, improve sleep, and reduce depression and aggression. In one study at the Renfrew Center, a residential eating disorder treatment facility in Florida, research indicated that music therapy provided individually and in large and small groups was effective in motivating eating disorder patients. The finding showed that it enhanced their positive affect about the recovery process and was well received.

How to Incorporate Music Therapy

If your counselor, physician, or other health care provider does not know a music therapist, EDreferral.com provides a list of professionals who may offer a coordinated program of music and music therapy interventions. If you are interested in locating a music therapist, contact the American Music Therapist Association at *findMT@musictherapy.org* or call (301) 589-3300. The AMTA national office staff can provide you with a current list of qualified music therapists in your local area.

 Question

How do I know someone is qualified?
Many individual therapies have professional bodies that represent the practitioners in their field and offer qualification standards needed for practitioners to meet in order to be a member.

Spiritual Support

There has been a great deal of research that suggests that, in general, people who have a sense of spirituality, or develop spirituality during times of crises, are more likely to have fewer incidences of mental disorders and are more likely to have a quicker recovery period when undergoing periods of psychological distress or life problems.

Why It Works

It is not clear why this is true, although some researchers have suggested that it may be partly due to the support from a close-knit faith community or that certain behaviors that often accompany a spiritual outlook, like meditation and prayer, may promote mental well-being by creating a calm and peaceful space. Singing spiritual hymns or reading related material may also create those same feelings of calm. In doing so, those participants may be reducing their own tendencies toward anxiety and depression.

In one study of 250 college-aged women, researchers concluded that those participants who stated they had strong spiritual and/or religious beliefs were more likely to rely on prayer, meditation, or spiritually or religiously oriented literature to cope with their body image distress, which they found effective. In contrast, participants in the study who did not have strong spiritual or religious beliefs were more likely to use various distractions, which were not deemed as effective in helping them deal with body image concerns.

How It Works

Certainly no one would advocate adopting a spiritual perspective in order to tackle an eating disorder, but if a child or teenager has an interest in or an affinity for a spiritual perspective, then it may well be an activity you'll want to encourage to help create a positive relationship to psychological well-being and for anger, anxiety, and depression management. When you are making decisions about treatment, you may decide to look for professional therapists and educators who share a similar affinity for your faith tradition or at least are knowledgeable enough that they can respect you or your child's beliefs even if the belief is not shared by the professionals.

By the same token, if a child is struggling with an eating disorder and the child also chooses to reject the spiritual beliefs of his or her own family, then parents may need to decide what they are willing and able to fight for. You may decide that your family requires all members to go to a worship service but not various additional group activities. Do not engage in spiritual arguments or debates with your child if he or she disagrees with your own beliefs. Instead, listen, offer support, and focus on the overall health of your child.

Twelve-Step Programs

Many people are unaware of twelve-step groups beyond those for alcoholics. In fact, AA, or Alcoholics Anonymous, is the most well-known and the original twelve-step support group. The program evolved from a group called the Oxford Group, which had a Christian orientation and, at the time, used only six steps instead of twelve. AA was founded in 1937, based on the idea that alcoholics could not maintain sobriety alone, but they could stay sober through daily accountability to each other. This sense of accountability became one of the cornerstones of AA. Eventually, another key concept was added—that of sponsorship. Some members who have more experience with recovery would sponsor, or mentor, new members. From those AA meetings have sprung dozens of support groups for almost any addiction one can imagine, including disordered eating.

Why It Works

Overeaters Anonymous, or OA, boasts over 9,000 weekly meetings in fifty countries, and it addresses compulsive and binge eating. According to the Twelve Steps and Twelve Traditions of Overeaters Anonymous (1998), the only requirement for OA membership "is a desire to stop eating compulsively." However, over the past several years, OA members have warmly welcomed those people who suffer from other eating disorders, including bulimia and anorexia.

How It Works

Overeaters Anonymous meetings can be found all over the country, and teenagers are welcomed. Meetings are free, although a donation may be given. In a typical hour-long meeting, a meditation is read and members go around the room and introduce themselves. Business is taken care of, and there may be a guest speaker or a leader may share from his or her own experiences or from the OA literature. Sharing is voluntary, and many people find the meetings to be warm and supportive. Participants are encouraged to share their phone numbers and e-mail addresses with one another and to call for support when needed. For those who live in larger, more metropolitan areas such as Los Angeles and the San Fernando Valley in California, there are twelve-step meetings designed specifically for those people who have anorexia and/or bulimia.

Yoga and Other Movement Activities

Dance and movement therapists focus on improving body image, self-esteem, nonverbal communication through movement, and coping strategies for stress management. Yoga has been demonstrated to improve anxiety, depression, stress, body esteem, self-esteem, physical health, well-being, and chronic pain. People with eating disorders are disconnected from their bodies, and the advantage of yoga is that it helps them to reconnect, offering moments of "being okay" in their bodies. Yoga has been proven to:

- Improve body awareness
- Create a greater responsiveness to bodily sensations
- Promote greater body satisfaction
- Lower self-objectification
- Increase reflective ability
- Improve ability to self-soothe

 Fact

Mind-body exercise, such as yoga, has been proven to be associated with greater body satisfaction and fewer symptoms of eating disorders than traditional aerobic exercise like cardio machines or jogging.

How It Works

Susi Costello, RN, teaches yoga to many people with eating disorders. "Yoga is probably helpful because, in its true, authentic form it defines a really healthy, balanced lifestyle. It's developing a nonviolent, compassionate mind-set toward yourself and the world;

it's learning to breathe in a way that minimizes anxiety, increases health; it helps you look at life in an entirely different way, unlike the "typical" way people think and act—for instance, ignoring and avoiding the things you don't like, the things that make you uncomfortable—yoga practice allows you to be comfortable with the parts of life that you don't love. You actually can tolerate sadness, anger, anxiety . . . it's not that you love it, you just realize it's part of your life, plus you know it'll change pretty soon. You know the good stuff changes pretty soon too, so you totally enjoy it while it's there."

CHAPTER 14

Good Nutrition Is Medicine

An ED patient gets worse every day if he or she isn't getting 100 percent of his or her nutritional needs met. And every day the patient doesn't get 100 percent of what he or she needs, it gets harder to for the child to become healthier. Food is not only fuel for the body, it is fuel for the brain. If your child isn't eating well, then your child's brain isn't going to work well. That means all the counseling in the world isn't going to help if the brain isn't working right.

Setting Priorities

The therapeutic process in healing your child's eating disorder must include good nutrition, and it must include the child's family. Sending a child away to a residential treatment center and returning her to the family without empowering the child's family to maintain good nutrition is useless, as is spending hours in therapy if a child is so malnourished that none of the information can get in.

Family Matters

Even with the best dietitian in the world, a good nutritional plan is useless unless the child actually eats the food. The family, particularly Mom and Dad, or the primary caregiver, has a unique opportunity and obligation to make sure that the child eats. After all, it was Mom and Dad who made sure their child ate as an infant and has been there from the first bottle and the first spoonful of baby cereal to offering the first messy slice of birthday cake. Who better to help their child become healthy once again?

 Essential

> As parents, you can offer a lot to your child. You can offer support, safety, and even a great deal of sympathy. But what you cannot do is provide a safe harbor for your child's eating disorder. That means there is no room for compromise when it comes to full nutrition. No safe harbor.

Claiming Your Role

In the not so good old days of eating disorder treatment, counselors and physicians were very intentional about keeping parents in the dark about the care of their child. After all, parents were blamed for their children's eating disorder. In some situations, they still are. It only makes sense that if parents are to blame for their child's eating disorder, then why allow them to have a say in their child's treatment? Under this outdated model, the only participation parents have is in opening up the checkbook and paying whatever the professionals ask.

Why You Must Take Control

Somebody is going to be in control in your family. If it isn't you as a parent, then it's your child. And if your child has disordered eating, than it's the eating disorder that will begin to take over. "I feel like a prisoner in my own house. Almost every decision we make in our family, from finances to dinner, revolves around Anna," explains a frustrated mom. "And I know people think we shouldn't give her so much power and control, but she could die. If I don't cater to her, she could die from the disease."

Understand the Risks

The longer a child has an eating disorder, the more difficult it is to treat. That means that allowing a child and her eating disorder to run a house simply feeds the eating disorder. After all, the child wants power and control because he feels out of control, and now, even if it is uncomfortable, with an eating disorder he has the power to run a household. That also means the longer your child holds on to the eating disorder, the more of a death grip it will have on your child.

Stopping the Behavior

Effective treatment means parents must learn to modify a child's self-destructive behaviors. James Lock, MD, PhD, coauthor of *Help Your Child Beat an Eating Disorder*, explains, "If you had a son or daughter who drank a couple of cups of vodka every morning before school, you would probably stop that behavior. You would find a way. This behavior—starving yourself, for example, to the degree that people with anorexia nervosa do—is so dangerous and so hazardous that it is really comparable, and perhaps even more dangerous, than drinking shots before school. Regardless of the cause, the behavior itself is the problem. You have to stop the behavior."

Setting Appropriate Goals

Parents must effectively encourage their children to eat enough food to gain and/or maintain a weight that is healthy for their own body. Do not worry about setting a weight goal yet. Focus on short-term goals and reversing the malnutrition. That is the primary focus at first.

No Compromise

"One of the most important things I learned in helping my son to eat was to set a goal, and to not compromise. My son had to eat a certain amount of food within a certain amount of time. He soon learned that if it wasn't eaten, nothing else was going to happen. We learned from other parents that what worked best was that after an amount of time has passed—and it was a time period we had chosen in advance and informed him of—we give him the option: drink the equivalent amount of calories in a meal replacement beverage or we leave the house. If he won't drink, then we take him out of the house and go to the hospital for a feeding via an NG tube. It only took one trip to the hospital parking lot before he realized that we would not give the eating disorder a safe harbor."

Starting from Scratch

Taking control of your child's eating requires a new set of ground rules. You are intervening to refuse to allow the voice of the eating disorder to make decisions for your child about what will or will not be eaten. That means, whether your child is nine or seventeen, you as the caregiver are making the rules about food—all of them. Your child cannot be allowed to make any decisions on eating until body and mind are healing. The primary caregiver who is in charge of meals now makes all decisions regarding food.

A New Set of Rules

If your child enjoyed being in the kitchen—planning meals and cooking and preparing meals for the family—that stops now. In some ways, dealing with food in those ways satisfied the desire to eat. Obviously, the next right decision is to take away that satisfaction.

Your child no longer has the burden of dealing with food, other than eating it. That will be enough of a task. Calories are now an off-limits conversation. You are going to prepare your child's meals and make decisions about calories and content without any input from your child.

"My child would ask before meals, 'What are we having for lunch?' It would sound like a normal topic of conversation, but I could tell it was a desperate attempt to start focusing and planning, even though there wasn't anything she could do about it. I learned to say, 'I'm not sure yet,' even if I was getting ready to put food on the plate. She knew what she was eating when it was placed before her. When she asked how many calories she was eating or an overview of the meal plan, especially for the first several months, all I said was, 'It's what you need to be healthy.' I probably said it a hundred times the first few weeks," reports one mother.

Magic Plate

"I loved the concept of the Magic Plate that is used in the Maudsley method. It worked well for us, though I admit it was tiring, especially at first," said Anne, the mother of a daughter with anorexia. The concept of the Magic Plate is that your child no longer has a say in what goes in her mouth. Three times a day (or snacks, too, if necessary), a plate appears in front of her. The rule is simple: what you put in front of your child must be eaten within a specific time period. The calorie level will vary depending on your child's needs, but typically the calorie count is high.

The Plan

Once a meal is placed in front of your child at the table, nothing happens unless the meal is eaten. Nothing. This will likely be the hardest part of restoring nutrition to your child. Your child cannot go to school, go to work, go play, use the phone, or do anything unless the meal is eaten. There will be times when you as the caregiver will want to run out of the door even more than your child does, so prepare now for some long meals. Some parents set a time limit that the meal has to be eaten in; others don't, but say if the meal isn't eaten in a certain time frame, then a trip to the hospital is in order.

"My child was eating a few hundred calories a day on the days he was eating at all. When I took over, I set an initial calorie goal and did not tell him what it was. I simply prepared his plate in the other room, placed it in front of him, and let him know that my expectations were that he would eat it all. He was so angry that the first night he threw his meal across the room. I got up and made another plate of food without even responding to the outburst. I learned for the first week or two at least to make extra food just in case. I also had to get my brother-in-law to stand in the dining room and block the door. He never touched my son; he just blocked the way so my son could not leave. He had to deal with the food. After a few days, it was a relief. He could eat because he didn't want to, but it wasn't his choice anymore. The most incredible thing was that I could see a difference in his mental health in only a few days. It took almost seven months to regain the thirty-five pounds he had lost, but I could see progress in his mental stability every week. Remember—this is a long haul," asserts Mona, whose son has been recovered from his eating disorder for over three years.

Question

Should I reward my child for eating?
It's a bad habit to get into, and rewards rarely work. You can promise everything you can afford and then some, but the only incentive to offer for eating needs to be the ability to have a life, such as getting to go to school or be with friends.

Stages

Typically, for a family-based eating plan, there are a series of stages that families will go through in healing their child, in restoring a healthy weight, and in helping their child to make good and healthy decisions about food and activity on their own. Stage one typically starts with the child losing all control of meals and what will be eaten, and this can continue for several months, at least until weight restoration is progressing well.

 **Essential**

If your child is at a friend's house or family member's during meal-times, then plan ahead of time. Speak with the adult ahead of time and explain what is happening. Send along an appropriate meal and tell the adult when it needs to be eaten. Ask them to call you when the meal is completed. If it isn't eaten, go and get your child.

Stage two is a transition for when a child is ready to have at least one snack on her own. All other meals and snacks are supervised. "I had to learn that this is a long haul. After a few weeks of stage one, I thought my daughter might be ready for stage two, so I gave her a large bowl of two servings of cherries (about 1½ cups) and said, 'This is the fruit for breakfast and lunch. Eat what you want now and then you can eat the rest for lunch.' It was a disaster. She freaked. She tried to count them out so she could know exactly how many she could have and it would still be okay. I knew we weren't ready yet." By the end of the second stage, you should see significant progress in your child's overall health and well-being, in addition to her attitude and willingness to eat. The third stage focuses more on establishing an identity separate from the eating disorder.

How to Take Charge

Anytime a parent decides to take charge of an eating disorder, you can expect the child to panic. In fact, the child's behavior and disordered eating may even get worse at first. Prepare yourself for screaming tempter tantrums, outright hatred, and cold fear. All of a sudden, when parents take control of the disease, much of the child's life is now out of her control and it doesn't feel good to your child. It's the same as if you were taking your child to chemotherapy and he was vomiting for hours afterward, but you know it was the only way to save his life—you'd make the difficult decision for his long-term health.

 **Question**

What do I do about school?
Either go to school and eat with your child inside or have your child eat in the car with you. If that isn't a possibility, meet with the principal and ask your child to eat every meal with the school nurse. Have the nurse call you if the meal is not eaten completely.

Weigh-ins

If you are working with a medical provider, then he or she may suggest some guidelines about regular weigh-ins. If so, then you may decide to only allow your child to be weighed during those appointments. Make sure those weigh-ins are blind, meaning that your child cannot see the weight on the scale, nor see the weight being recorded. The child should stand backward on the scale during the weigh-in. In addition, the child should be surprised by most weigh-ins, without allowing your child time to binge on water to "fool" the scale.

 Essential

Keep your scale at home locked up so your child does not have access to it. If your child regularly goes to friends' houses, have a conversation with them and ask them to put away their scales as well. It can be embarrassing, but it's better than trying to undo the damage later.

Social Media

What young person goes anywhere without a cell phone these days? It keeps a child from being isolated and helps them connect with friends, and you can keep track of your child. It can also be a tool used to count calories, encourage other people with eating disorders via text or calls, or use Facebook or e-mail to get pro–eating disorder inspiration. Create rules that work for your family. Use the phone as a reward for eating, but make sure you have a cell plan that allows you to read every text that comes in or out and then use it. Track your child's computer use. If she is using a calorie counter to track her meals, then make her stop by whatever means necessary.

Body Checking

For a person with an eating disorder, a mirror, especially a large or full-length one, can be an enemy. People with eating disorders can become obsessed with looking in the mirror, looking for flaws, and then reacting because of the flaws they see, or they may see some progress and be encouraged to continue. Use your best judgment about the availability of mirrors in the house, though many families put away all full-length mirrors and cover all but one bathroom mirror. Body checking can also occur with string, measuring tape, cell phone cameras, and scales. If you take away the opportunities to compare, some of the momentum behind the constant checking can be minimized.

 Essential

Websites that promote anorexia and bulimia, often called "pro-ana" sites, offer places where users can encourage one another in unhealthy eating behaviors. Track which sites your child visits and, if necessary, block access to a computer unless accompanied by an adult.

What Does My Child Need?

You have to eat a certain number of calories per day just to stay alive and functioning. After all, it takes calories to support breathing, a heart beat, and blood circulation. Then you need to factor in the amount of calories needed to maintain your child's current weight.

A teenager, for example, may need 1,800–2,000 calories per day, depending on weight and height and the amount of activity. Then factor in the amount of calories your child needs to gain weight.

 Fact

Remember, metabolism will speed up as calories are increased, and you will need to adjust calories accordingly.

Calorie Requirements

The following table lists the estimated amounts of calories needed to maintain energy balance for various gender and age groups at three different levels of physical activity. The estimates are rounded to the nearest 200 calories and were determined using the Institute of Medicine equation.

Gender	Age (years)	Activity Level		
		Sedentary	Moderately Active	Active
Female	2–3	1,000	1,000-1,400	1,000–1,400
	4–8	1,200	1,400–1,600	1,400–1,800
	9–13	1,600	1,600–2,000	1,800–2,200
	14–18	1,800	2,000	2,400
	19–30	2,000	2,00–2,200	2,400
	31–50	1,800	2,000	2,200
	51+	1,600	1,800	2,000-2,200
Male	4–8	1,400	1,400–1,600	1,600–2,000
	9–13	1,800	1,800–2,200	2,000–2,600
	14–18	2,200	2,400–2,800	2,800–3,200
	19–30	2,400	2,600–2,800	3,000
	31–50	2,200	2,400–2,600	2,800–3,000
	51+	2,000	2,200–2,400	2,400–2,800

Source: *www.health.gov/dietaryguidelines/dga2005/document/html/chapter2.htm*

Track It

Many parents find that a software program like Dietpower (*www.dietpower.com*) can be useful in keeping track of your child's calories. Typically, it is used for dieting, but it can also be used for weight gain and maintenance. It provides helpful charts and expected target dates for weight goals, and it retails for about $50.00. There may be other software programs as well as websites that would be helpful. Plus, the Mastercook series of cookbooks is an excellent source of recipes that offer a dietary profile of each meal and can help with meal planning.

No Blinking

Parents must find the support they need to stay strong during meals. Parents must treat each meal as critical and refuse to allow a child to leave the table until the meal is completed. Focus on the plan that nothing else can happen until your child is at 100 percent of his or her nutritional goals and everything else is secondary. Patience, firm boundaries, and clear expectations can be comforting to your child's lost inner child. The eating disorder, however, will find it frustrating and will fight against it. Be ready.

What Do I Feed My Child?

"My daughter was so very small, and we started feeding her 3,000 calories per day for the first three months of refeeding. The best thing we did was make our magic milkshake. We took two or three scoops of the highest-calorie premium ice cream, added a cup of full-fat milk, and a scoop of protein powder," suggests one mom. High-calorie foods are the best choices during refeeding.

Sample Meal Plans

Following are some sample meal plans:

BREAKFAST
¾ cup dry cereal + ¼ cup nuts + ¼ cup dried fruit
1 cup whole milk or fortified soymilk
1 large banana

SNACK
12 crackers
2 ounces cheese
½ cup orange juice

LUNCH
Sandwich: 2 slices bread + 3 ounces tuna or deli meat + ⅛
    avocado + lettuce/tomato
8 ounces yogurt
Trail mix: ½ cup pretzels + ¼ cup nuts + ¼ cup dried fruit
1 cup juice

SNACK
½ cup hummus
8 olives
½ cup carrot sticks
1 pita

DINNER
4 ounces salmon
1 cup couscous
½ cup vegetables sautéed in oil
1 cup salad + 1 tablespoon dressing
1 cup whole milk

SNACK
3 cups popcorn with butter + salt
1 cup whole milk

Meal Ideas

2 omelets with cream cheese, bacon, or sausage

2 packets instant oatmeal

2 cups cereal (nuts mixed in)

Fetticini Alfredo with peas and chicken

2 slices bread, 4 ounces turkey, mayo, yogurt smoothie, carrots, and hummus

1 large baked potato with butter, cheese, sour cream, bacon

Beverages

White or chocolate whole milk with whey protein

Soy, rice, or almond milk

Juice

Ensure

Instant shake packets with whole milk

Super Snack Ideas

- A large bagel with 3 tablespoons almond butter (almost 600 calories)
- Protein bars (about 300 calories per bar)
- Mixed nuts (1 ounce=170 calories)
- Large bakery muffins
- Hostess apple pies
- Corn bread
- Gourmet coffee drinks
- Chips with sour-cream-based dip
- Nutella milkshakes
- Fresh fruit with honey sauce
- Carrot sticks with hummus
- Brownie with whipped cream
- S'mores
- Premium ice cream smoothie
- Yogurt with fruit and granola

- Faux banana split (consisting of 1¼ cups yogurt (full-fat kind), ½ cup granola, walnuts, chocolate syrup, banana, strawberries

 Fact

Zinc supplementation of anorexia nervosa patients has been reported to increase the weight gain during the refeeding process. Talk to your health care provider about the recommended dosage.

Is This Healthy?

Forget what you learned about nutrition. For this project, unless your child is struggling with obesity, bring back the butter, whole milk, whole yogurt, skin-on chicken, and sauces. Serve premium ice cream with strawberries and whipped cream.

Some supplements can serve double duty—restore depleted vitamins and minerals and boost calorie counts. For example, some flaxseed capsules (high in omega-3) are 70 calories each. Talk to your health care provider about any nutritional supplements you use.

 Fact

Think mini treats. One calorie-dense, bite-sized snack is easier to get down than 2 cups of pudding.

This Is Miserable!

No parent whose son or daughter has an eating disorder will argue with you. Refeeding your child is not a pleasant task. Expect your child to resist. Expect to encounter any number of these behaviors:

- Screaming curses
- Throwing things
- Hurting themselves
- Hurting others
- Running away

No Shortcuts

There is no shortcut to recovery. There are, however, lots of paths to worse illness, disability, and death. Those are the stakes you're dealing with—every time you sit down for dinner. Refeeding is hard, but losing a child to an eating disorder is even more difficult. To be clear, while it is possible for a child with an eating disorder to be cured, refeeding is not a guarantee of a cure. It is, however, one of the best ways you have to get your child on the road toward recovery.

Encouragement

Many parents find this to be a difficult time, and they need encouraging words to make it through. At the same time, they need to give encouraging words to their children who are also struggling. Some of these phrases have been helpful to other parents and children in recovery:

"It's not your fault."
"When in charge, be in charge."
"Food is medicine."
"Life stops until you eat."
"If something isn't working, it needs to change."
"It's a marathon, not a sprint."
"Put on your own oxygen mask first."
"Change the behavior and the mind will follow."
"I love you too much to let this illness take you away. We won't leave you, and we won't give up. We're here."

CHAPTER 15

When Disagreements Occur

The blessing of having an interdisciplinary team is that you have access to a wealth of resources, education, information, and advice. The drawback to having such an assembly of professionals walking with you is that there are times when there will be conflict. Sometimes you will disagree with their recommendations or they will disagree with one another, and you will be forced to make difficult decisions based on your own research, intimate knowledge of your own child, and intuition.

The Nature of Disagreements

When you have a child with an eating disorder, many people will have ideas, suggestions, and outright demands on what you should do, when you should do it, and who you should do it with. Expect people around you, including parents, partners, friends, extended family members, physicians, and other members of an interdisciplinary treatment team, to have strongly held opinions that may or may not be based on facts, and expect to disagree with some of those opinions. In other words, not everyone around you will agree with each other, with you, with treatment decisions, or even with how recovery ought to be measured.

Navigating Disagreements

Disagreements can be handled in a number of ways:

- One person may either agree that the other person is right or at least agrees to accept the other's decision.
- A third way can be found, accepting neither person's choice but finding a different solution altogether.
- The person who has the power makes the decision and the other person remains adamantly opposed to the decision and may fight against it.
- The disagreement is so difficult that no decision is made, and no action is taken. For a child with an eating disorder, this response can have deadly consequences.

Disagreement Resolution

For the most part, disagreements need to be worked through, and they can successfully be managed. Here is an example: your child has a therapist who initially agreed to use a family-centered approach to treating your child's eating disorder. However, as months have passed, you have begun to realize that the therapy does not focus as much on wellness and recovery as it does on self-exploration and expressing one's feelings. When you speak with the therapist about coming together and doing family work, you are put off again and again. What does a parent do?

First, speak to the provider. Make an appointment for yourself and sit down and discuss your concerns. Clearly explain what is wrong, what you need to see change, and listen carefully to the provider's response. It may be that your perception was inaccurate and that you wish to continue working with the provider. Or, it may be that you no longer wish to have this person working with your child. If so, you may explain your decision, but you should ask what you need to do to terminate the relationship and have copies of your child's records.

Fact

Even if your child likes his therapist and has developed a good rapport with her, you cannot continue the therapy if the therapy goals are not being met in a mutually agreed on way or if you are being excluded from the therapeutic process. Continuing with a therapist who is a bad fit for you and your family will simply do additional harm to your child.

When Professionals Disagree

It is the nature of the beast: put a handful of health care providers —a counselor, a nutritionist, a physician, and psychiatrist—in the same room, and you are likely looking at an incredibly diverse array of experience, education, philosophies, and personal beliefs. Expecting them all to agree all of the time would be naïve and probably won't happen. It is important to keep in mind that all of the providers you come in contact with are going to provide you with the best information they have available to them at the time. It may not be up to date, and it may not even be accurate, but they do believe that what they are suggesting is the best way to help your child.

Reach Out

When you have professionals on your treatment team who disagree with one another, with your research, or with you, the ability to find support, encouragement, and information from the wider eating disorder community becomes absolutely critical. If you have a group of well-educated and informed families, former patients, and providers by your side, you are better able to withstand any pushback you receive as well as sort out any conflicting information you are given.

"For me, being in contact with the larger national organizations for eating disorders made all the difference in the world. By linking up with them, I suddenly had an entire world of information at my fingertips and I was no longer dependent on the narrow-minded, outdated perspectives that my daughter's pediatrician offered. I needed a place to turn when I knew what the doctor or counselor said was just wrong or when their statements conflicted with each other," added Laney, mother of a child with bulimia.

Living with Disagreement

In an ideal world, everyone on your team of providers, from your doctor to the therapist to the nutritionist and counselor, would all be on the same page regarding every aspect of your child's care. While you're dreaming, everyone else in your life is patting you on the back and agreeing that the path you've chosen and the professionals you've picked are the best in the field. If you want to dream big, even your child agrees with the treatment plan and is pleasant, willing, and ready to give up the eating disorder and resume a normal, happy, and healthy childhood.

It probably isn't going to happen that way. It is likely that there will be times when members of the team you've put together do not agree with one another or with you. This is when it is critical to keep the big picture in mind. If the physician doesn't agree with the counselor's approach, but is comfortable with her role as primary care provider in terms of monitoring your child's health, then agreeing to disagree may be acceptable. If team members express a disagreement about another treatment approach, make sure you ask questions so you clearly understand their concerns, thank them for their caring concern, and let them know you will give their opinion careful consideration. Your team members do not have to agree as long as your child's care is not compromised.

When You Disagree with the Hospital

Sometimes when a child has an eating disorder, a hospital visit is required, either for psychiatric inpatient care or to stabilize the child medically. However, once your child is admitted, you might disagree

with the treatment plan. For example, your daughter was hospitalized for dehydration, and after a week of intravenous fluids and careful monitoring, she is physically stable. However, the hospital wants
to keep your daughter for another week. The hospital psychiatrist
wants her to have more intensive inpatient therapy on the adolescent
psychiatric unit. You prefer her to see the counselor she's been working with. You are concerned that more treatment with a new therapist will muddy the already murky waters. Now what?

Who Gets to Decide?

If the hospital believes your child's physical health is at risk by
refusing its services, you may have a fight on your hands. They may
threaten to use legal means to force you to keep your child there.
There are some important considerations when handling a con-
frontation with hospital staff:

- **Be calm.** Even if you are furious or terrified, yelling or making
  threats will undermine your credibility and may get you
  removed from the hospital by the police—without your child.
- **Listen carefully.** Make sure you understand their concerns
  and what they want to happen.
- **Don't waste your breath.** If the nurse is passing along information from a physician, for example, don't argue with the
  nurse. She has no power to change the physician's orders.
  Instead, speak with the physician directly.
- **Ask for a patient advocate.** Most hospitals have a patient representative or advocate, or a social worker, who has experience mediating such concerns. You may need to request a
  care plan conference, which typically involves the advocate, admitting physician, and other interested parties,
  including the parents.
- **Ask if there are other ways the hospital's concerns can be
  met.** For example, if they believe your child needs more
  intensive psychological support, can your child's therapist

or psychiatrist agree to see the child within twenty-four hours and provide a faxed document saying so?

- **Ask what happens next.** This is an important question. You need to ask the hospital what action it will take if you fail to give consent for the treatment plan they want for your child. In some cases, if you remove your child, the hospital will call CPS, or child protective services, and report you for medical neglect.

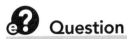 ## Question

Can the hospital stop me from taking my son home?
Yes, but it isn't likely. In some rare cases, if a hospital feels that you will be harming your child physically by taking him home, they can petition to remove your rights to make medical decisions for the child. It isn't likely, but it is possible.

Against Medical Advice

When you disagree with a hospital treatment plan, you do have the option to remove your child from the facility against medical advice, or AMA. However, you need to understand that a significant problem with taking your child from the hospital against medical advice is that your insurance company may decide not to cover any of the previous hospital stay, even if it was medically necessary treatment.

 ## Fact

If you sign out against medical advice, your physician will usually decide not to accept your child as a patient again. While that may be fine with you, if you live in an area with limited resources, you may need to take that into consideration.

If you are considering such an action, first call your insurance company to determine its policy regarding signing out against medical advice. Sometimes insurance companies will automatically decline to pay for any portion of the treatment, or they may wait until a claim is submitted by the hospital and then review it once all of the information has been received. This process can take weeks or even months before a decision is made. If you do check out against medical advice, make sure you take copies of all relevant paperwork home with you, or file a request for copies in case you need to argue your case later.

 Essential

If you remove your child against medical advice and the hospital says it will call child protective services for doing so, contacting an attorney with experience in this area may well be worth it. If CPS shows up at your door demanding custody of your child, you want someone you can call immediately.

Not Enough Treatment

Disagreements with hospitals often stem from parents refusing to consent to a treatment plan. There are, however, times when you want the hospital or another health care provider to do something and they refuse. What then? Again, the patient advocate can be a helpful resource for you. Again, listen carefully to the hospital's perspective and then state your case clearly, succinctly, and with as much hard evidence as you can provide. If you do not have health insurance or your insurance will not cover treatment, they cannot refuse to treat your child if his or her life is at stake. They can, however, stabilize your child and then transfer him or her to another hospital that may accept uninsured or underinsured patients.

 **Essential**

When Your Child Refuses Treatment

Since the nature of eating disorders usually lend themselves to a denial of said disorder, teens rarely welcome offered treatment and may attempt to refuse treatment altogether. Can a teenager decide to refuse treatment? With an adult, the health care system places a high value on autonomy, which recognizes that a competent individual has the right to make an informed choice about medical treatment, and the choice must be made without undue influences from others or coercion. With an eating disorder, two issues arise. First, do adolescents have the right to autonomy? If so, do patients with a serious psychiatric illness that may prove fatal if left untreated also retain their autonomy? The issues are complicated ones.

Reasons for Resistance

There are several reasons why a child may refuse eating disorder treatment:

- Fear of gaining weight
- The stigma of going to counseling or being hospitalized
- Concern that they will be the "craziest" or "fattest" person present
- Belief that nothing is wrong

The technical term for believing that nothing is wrong is anosognosia. In other words, the person with an eating disorder is simply unable to comprehend in her mind that she has a serious illness. Some brain injuries result in a similar condition, but with eating disorders, it is reversible with normalized eating and therapy.

Compassionate Intervention

A second principle that is key to understanding the health care system is the concept of beneficence. Beneficence requires that health care providers do what is considered to be "good" or in the best interests of the person for whom they provide care. Sometimes, providing good care may go against the wishes of a patient, particularly a minor child. However, the parents can play an important role in explaining what is going to happen, and why, and what will happen if the child cannot cooperate. There is no room for ambiguity regarding the parents' intention to require eating disorder treatment. One way the parents can convey that message is by explaining to their child that if outpatient therapy proves ineffective, then a higher level of care will be sought. The threat of being force-fed through a tube may well be an effective motivator.

The good news is that a minor has very few rights regarding the ability to refuse care, even for an eating disorder. *Compassionate intervention* is a term used to describe treating certain seriously ill people without their consent but in a way that seeks to understand the patient's choices, wishes, and goals. Most health care facilities and professionals will seek to give the young person as much autonomy as is reasonable.

Treatment teams can provide greater autonomy in these ways:

- Team members take into consideration the child's state of health, life experience, skills, and interests when planning care.
- Staff members listen to the young person's concerns and feedback concerning care and make adjustment as appropriate.
- The young person is encouraged to express her wishes, goals, and dreams, both long and short term.

Fact

Resistance in Adult Children

When a child with an eating disorder becomes a legal adult at eighteen, new issues emerge, including health insurance, confidentiality, and autonomy. Parents do not have any legal authority to force their child into treatment once their child turns eighteen, even if the child is still in high school and still living at home. An adult child with an eating disorder can feel even more overwhelming to parents simply because he has fewer treatment options available.

Involuntary Commitment

There are some legal avenues you can use to have your adult child involuntarily committed, but it is not necessarily an easy process. If this is an option you wish to consider pursuing, contact the social worker or intake person at the facility you have chosen for treatment. Studies show that adult patients who are involuntarily committed for an eating disorder generally require a longer stay than those who voluntarily choose to enter treatment, often because they start out in worse health. However, even those who are involuntarily committed often do well in the long term.

 Essential

It is possible to pressure your adult child into entering treatment by removing different means of support, such as financial help, if she refuses to comply. If you are considering this option, create a plan with your child's counselor or your own.

Health Insurance

Your adult child may still be on your health insurance and medical treatment may be covered until your child is twenty-one. This may depend on whether your child is enrolled in college. Your coverage may depend on several factors, including ever-changing federal laws as well as the limitations and exclusions on your own health insurance policy.

Confidentiality

If you haven't heard of HIPAA yet, you will soon. The Health Insurance Portability and Accountability Act of 1996 is a federal law that provides a means to protect individuals' medical records from becoming public knowledge. What that means for parents is that once your child becomes an adult, even if you are paying for her health insurance, you cannot talk with health professionals or facilities without your child's written permission. However, if you get a written power of attorney, anyone with a power of attorney can sign legal documents for the patient and read or transport medical records in the patient's absence.

Legal Matters

If your child is over eighteen, you are not your child's legal guardian unless you have been appointed by a court. If your child turns eighteen and is willing to give up his decision-making power regarding health care, then a legal document, such as a medical or durable power of attorney, or POA, can be enacted. Your child must agree to have such a document, and many young people are not willing to do so. If your child does not agree, you can petition the court to give you legal authority over him. The specific procedures will vary from state to state, but the key is this: if your child is over eighteen, you have no legal authority to force him into treatment.

Fact

Coping with Resistance

A lot of parents think that once they confront their child about the eating disorder, the child will tearfully agree it was a problem and then cheerfully agree to get help. After all, who wouldn't want to be healthy and happy? Most people with an active eating disorder don't see their disordered eating as a problem, much less a life-threatening disease. Resistance to treatment is the cornerstone of most eating disorders, and your child may resist your efforts in a wide variety of ways, including some you never thought were possible from your child.

He might be quietly passive, sneaking food or saying she already ate at a friend's house or at school, or she might be more actively resistant by simply refusing to eat at all. The spectrum of resistance can go all the way to extreme noncompliance and can include threats of suicide, self-injury, destruction of property, and extreme aggression toward others. What's a parent to do?

What Resistance Means

"When my son dug in his heels and refused to cooperate, it was exhausting. I am not going to lie. But other parents prepared me that it was going to be difficult. And one of the keys they taught me was that his strong refusal to cooperate did not mean that his mom and I were doing something wrong, In fact, the opposite was true. His resistance to our insistence on recovery and good health was the problem, not us. His resistance showed us just how sick he really was," offers Bryce, the father of a son with EDNOS (eating disorder not otherwise specified).

Essential

> When anxiety is running high and resistance is threatening to rear its ugly head, consider a distraction at the dinner table. Playing cards, chatting, even watching a video can allow your child to eat without focusing on the food.

It's this simple: healthy minds don't refuse healthy food. However, you cannot control whether or not your child resists. What you can control is your response to your child's resistance. For example, you can choose not to overreact to resistance. When faced with refusal, tears, or even yelling, ignore the behaviors and then firmly but kindly insist that there is no choice and the meal must be eaten.

Response to Resistance

Coping with your child's resistance regarding treatment and refeeding can be exhausting and time-consuming. Expect your child to be resistant to change. The only way to do it and stay healthy yourself is if you can recruit someone in your life—a friend, partner, family member—to help and support you throughout the process. With your child's treatment team, counselor, or physician, create a plan of action to put in place if your child's resistance becomes unmanageable to the point where your child isn't safe or is threatening the safety of others either by throwing things or making threats. Your plan may involve calling the police, going to the emergency room, or calling an ambulance.

 Fact

> Be prepared for your child's resistance. If your child dumps her food in the trash, have extra food available so you don't need to waste time in preparing more nutritious meals or snacks.

Holding Firm

Your confidence in your child's abilities can be very comforting for your child, even if the only outward emotion you see is anger and fear. Believe that your child has the capacity to heal from the eating disorder and that appropriate treatment and nourishment is mandatory for healing to occur. As such, participating in treatment is not optional, nor is eating. Accordingly, everything in your child's life—whether it is school, being with friends, or attending special events—must stop until your child eats what you have given him and keeps it down for a specific period of time afterward.

 Alert

Take threats of suicide seriously. If you can't ensure your child's safety 24/7, seek professional assistance immediately. Any patient at risk for suicide should be monitored by mental health care professionals

You may find it helpful to work together in counseling to create a contract for your child that clearly identifies expectations for him, what he can earn for compliance, and lose for noncompliance.

Change Happens

As the young person with an eating disorder moves through different stages of treatment, parents shouldn't be surprised to see the types and severity of resistance change over time. As medications are adjusted and treatment is ongoing, your child's actions and reactions will change, too. Recovery is rarely a straight road, and it often includes periods of a lack of motivation to change, frustration, relapse, as well as periods of improved wellness.

Resistance is best met with a collaborative treatment team that agrees together to present a unified front that refuses to allow the disease to continue and supports your child with every possible resource available.

CHAPTER 16

Help for the Parents

Parenting a child with an eating disorder is exhausting work, for you, for your child, and for your entire family. It may seem nearly impossible to find the strength not just to keep going but to take care of your other children, your work, and other primary relationships. Something needs to give. A parent's own struggles with an eating disorder, mental health issues, or other concerns may serve to make a difficult time only worse. While you might be able to keep it all together by yourself, why would you want to?

Self-Care

Seeing someone you love struggling with an eating disorder might make you feel very scared, angry, frustrated, and helpless. Helping your loved one work through the disorder is exhausting. Going to appointments, battling health insurance companies, wading through paperwork and bills, and trying to get your child to eat all somehow have to get done on top of regular life business.

"It has been rough," admits Robin. "I wish I hadn't isolated myself at the beginning. I was worried about what people would think if they knew about the eating disorder, so I pulled away from people who cared about me and my family. A few months into this, I recognized that we couldn't do it all by ourselves, so I finally started saying yes and accepted help—whether it was carpooling, babysitting, or just keeping me company at odd times.

"It might sound silly, but the world didn't end when I said yes. Life did get better. The eating disorder was still there, and my daughter was still struggling, but she also saw that there was this community of people who loved and cared about us—we didn't exist in a vacuum. I wish we weren't in that position, but at least we weren't alone."

 Alert

Be prepared to have to provide education about eating disorders to friends and loved ones, just as you would have to do with any life-threatening illness. You might want to print out resources from reputable online resources listed in Appendix C.

Acknowledge Needs

Without exception, parents of children with an eating disorder need support. Any parent whose child is sick needs help, and eating disorders are no less stressful or dangerous than many other diseases. To stay healthy, parents must intentionally look for ways to get their own needs for comfort, reassurance, relaxation, and rest met. Parents don't stop having needs when they start having children, and their needs don't stop when an eating disorder begins.

 Fact

Parents might well benefit from finding their own therapist to help guide them through this disease and to help them cope with the myriad of emotions that can arise when an eating disorder develops in the family.

Parents have an amazing capacity to show up when their child most needs them, particularly in a crisis. But once the immediate crisis passes, the parent is often left exhausted, physically and emotionally. Particularly if a parent doesn't have a partner, the experience can be very isolating. All parents of children with eating disorders must find another adult whom they can rely on and confide in to stay as healthy as possible. At the very least, parents must have someone who can provide an empathetic ear. They can also find strength in support groups for families with a loved one with mental illness.

 Essential

"Many mothers feel severely pressured these days. They often feel like they're falling short in one part, if not in several parts, of their lives. They often feel like they're failures. Well, people aren't failures when they're doing the best they can. Our performance doesn't have to be measured against anyone else's—just against our own abilities to cope." —Mister Fred Rogers

Changing Perspectives

When a child has a long-term illness like an eating disorder, it requires parents to focus on being aware of their thinking habits and then developing and maintaining more effective ones. For some parents, it may mean giving up the expectation of a perfectly clean house because, for now, dealing with an eating disorder is time-consuming. Another approach may be to hire a local college student to come in and clean once a week. Other thinking patterns that may be harmful include ones that either take on blame for the child's eating disorder, such as "I should have noticed it sooner," or "If I hadn't gotten a divorce, she wouldn't have stopped eating," or start assigning blame elsewhere. Thinking "My daughter could get over this if she wanted to" or "This is all my ex's fault for not being a better parent" may make you feel better for the moment, but it doesn't create a healthier you.

Share the Pain

Twelve-step groups have an expression: "Pain shared is pain halved." The idea behind the slogan is that when you share your pain with someone else who has been there and survived, you can feel hopeful about your own situation. It can be helpful to have someone else agree that, yes, the current situation is horrible and feels hopeless, but it doesn't stay horrible forever. Once you have secured a treatment team to address the child's needs and together you have created a treatment plan (family-based treatment, individual therapy, or inpatient hospitalization), then you need to find your own source of emotional support.

A Shared Path

"When I went to the support group for parents of children with eating disorders, the first time I talked to another mom about my daughter's binge eating, I felt like I could breathe for the first time in months. Finally, someone understood me. There was someone I could talk to that I didn't have to explain everything to. The support group is something that's for me."

Support groups can meet in person at local churches, hospitals, or physicians' offices. Parents who live near metropolitan areas are more likely to have access to in-person support groups, and they are typically free or low in cost. They are often led by a licensed therapist or counselor who may set guidelines for the group. Contact the education department of your closest hospital, or children's hospital if you live near one, to see if they offer support groups for parents or if they know where to locate one.

Unless hosted by a treatment facility, members of a support group may not approach treatment the same way that you do. You might want to ask the group facilitator if there is a preferred treatment method in the group. After all, if you are surrounded by people who disagree with your family's treatment plan, the experience may not be as beneficial as you would like.

Online Support

Particularly if parents do not live near an in-person support group, an online support group may be the next best resource. On online forums, participation is usually free, though it has its own set of governing guidelines. Online support forums typically offer a number of different topics where participants can usually read and post anonymously.

Research indicates that, for parents, the benefits of participating in online support groups can include:

- Being better informed
- Feeling more confident about their treatment plan
- Improved understanding of the disease
- Increased optimism
- Enhanced self-esteem and social well-being

 Essential

One of the best online forums is found on the F.E.A.S.T. (Families Empowered and Supporting Treatment for Eating Disorders) website, an online community of parents of eating disorder patients around the world. A well-monitored site, it limits participation to parents and caregivers, and it offers advice, support, and encouragement all based on the family-centered treatment approach (*www.feast-ed.org/ Forum.aspx*).

Protect the Parents' Relationship

Money battles, in-laws, and other issues of married life are difficult enough. But when your child has an eating disorder, it can create a significant amount of stress on the parents' relationship. Research shows that relationships affected by an ill child are affected by unexpected demands on parents' time, increased economic costs, and chronic grief. David Adams and Eleanor Deveau, in their book, *Coping with Childhood Cancer*, list several ways that parents can work together when they have a child with cancer. Granted, eating disorders are not the same as cancer, but they are both life-threatening diseases that affect the parents' relationship. Their suggestions include:

- Provide sympathy and understanding to each other instead of blame and criticism.
- Both parents must come together to learn about the diagnosis and treatment.
- Parents must share in caring and loving for their other children.
- Commit to sharing their own feelings of anger, sadness, sorrow, and hope with each other.
- Be willing to accept the help of family, friends, and neighbors.
- Trust their partners, and be loyal to them in the face of criticism or blame from relatives or others.

Old Patterns

Most couples have typical responses they tend to go back to when an argument begins. Sometimes, those roles can be along gender lines, others can just be habits born from years of use. For example, when faced with an eating disorder, men often withdraw, not out of a lack of caring, but out of a sense of powerlessness. They may spend more hours at work, or at least away from home. Women, who are often the primary caregivers for children, even if they work outside the home, may find it difficult to share decision-making or care-giving responsibilities. It is important to recognize which patterns are useful and which ones are not working for your situation.

"I am a take-charge person," admits Sonja, who applied that same approach to getting treatment for her son's eating disorder. "Sometimes I sort of sweep in and make decisions and then just inform my husband of what we're doing. While that might have been okay when I was planning the weekly schedule, it didn't work for Sam's treatment. I felt resentful and alone, and he felt excluded and unnecessary. It took a while for us to figure out what wasn't working, and counseling did help us sort it out."

 Question

How can I protect my relationship with my partner?
It is vital that the couple protects their relationship by spending time away, not only from the house, but from the eating disorder itself. Date nights can become important eating-disorder-free zones.

Get Real about Your Feelings

No parent holds a newborn baby for the first time and thinks, "I can't wait until this little angel grows up and starts hating her body, steals and gorges on food, then sticks a toothbrush down her throat to make herself vomit." When parents hear about it happening to other people's children, they often immediately think about the ways their child is different and how it will never happen to their family. But for too many families, it does happen.

I'm Disappointed

When an eating disorder develops in your child, it's disappointing. It's frustrating. "This is not our family," says Sam, whose daughter has battled bulimia on and off for several years. "We are not the kind of family that I thought had a daughter with bulimia. We weren't hypercritical; we didn't have any trauma or anything else I thought led to an eating disorder. All of a sudden, our daughter was sick and I was embarrassed, and mad at myself for being embarrassed.

"To make it worse, I was disappointed in my daughter. I never told her though, but I am sure she picked it up. I thought she was stronger than that. It took me a long time to realize that this wasn't something she could stop on her own. It's hard to admit that I felt that way about my child."

When It's Difficult to Like Your Child

When a child has an eating disorder, it is as though he or she was taken over by an alien. "It literally felt like my son was gone. The eating disorder completely took over his entire personality. It's like a year was just gone. He was distant, irritable, short-tempered, and just not very likeable," said Tom.

Guilt, fear, sorrow, anger, hopelessness, and confusion—having a child with an eating disorder creates a myriad of emotions, very few of them comfortable. Acknowledging that a child with an eating disorder may not be very likeable does not mean that you don't love your child. It does mean that you have real emotions in response to your child's behavior.

"What eventually helped me," explained Tom, "was when another parent told me to view this not-so-likeable part of my son as simply the eating disorder talking. What he was saying and doing, and even thinking, was not a part of who my son was, it was simply a manifestation of the neurobiological problem he carried. His actions didn't define my son any more than a cough would if he had a cold. When my son acted badly, instead of feeling defeated, I used that frustration to fuel the fight against the eating disorder."

Just Go Away

When faced with a difficult situation, each person copes the best way he or she can. When a person is emotionally aware and healthy, coping methods can often be healthy and include talking, crying, or turning to a source of spiritual support. At other times, parents may cope in maladaptive ways, whether it's eating, drinking, smoking, yelling, or even withdrawing. A child's behavior and attitudes can be so illogical and frustrating that the parent either responds in anger or by refusing to engage with the child at all.

Sometimes, withdrawing is purely about survival. Coping with an eating disorder is exhausting work. It can feel as though an eating disorder has taken the entire family hostage. Go too long without healthy space, and parents can grow to resent this very needy child. But withdraw too long and your child will feel even more isolated. Parents can also benefit from professional support separately from their children. As you know, parenting is all about love. But translating that love into parenting during a physical and mental illness like an eating disorder feels overwhelming. Ultimately, the bottom line is that your child needs you. Be aware of when you withdraw, and look for ways to make connections.

It's about Me

When a child has an eating disorder, the entire world seems to revolve around the child's disorder. Suddenly everything from the family schedule to the family budget and dinner table are all inexplicably intertwined with the disordered eating. Parents can feel as though they are living in the middle of a hurricane and simply don't have the luxury of taking care of themselves. That perspective can be dangerous to a parent's physical and emotional state.

Set Boundaries

Even if a parent is a therapist, physician, or psychologist, a parent cannot serve that role for a member of his or her family. A healthy parent must be able to set boundaries for what she can and cannot do when helping her child.

"I had to reserve one night a week for myself. My family knew that unless there is blood involved, Thursday night belongs to me. What I do has varied—sometimes I just go to the bookstore and drink coffee and read, other times I play tennis or get dinner with a friend. It feels good to have a meal where I can relax. When we were in the middle of refeeding, I had a family member stay at home in my place and all the rules stayed the same. It gave me something to look forward to when things at home got tense. Now things are much better, but I still carve out that time for myself to make sure I stay healthy."

Laughter Is Good for You

Nurture your sense of humor; it's true that laughter is sometimes the best medicine. Laughter relieves anxiety and depression and decreases stress hormones. Dr. Bernie Siegel, a cancer surgeon, wrote, "Laughter make the unbearable bearable, and a patient with a well-developed sense of humor has a better chance of recovery than a stolid individual who seldom laughs." How can you find ways to crack a smile when you just don't feel like it?

- Watch old comedies—think *I Love Lucy*, *Laurel and Hardy*, and *The Carol Burnett Show*.
- Play a game.
- Dig out bubbles, a yo-yo, even jacks or anything else that brings out the child in you.
- Pick up something funny to read or peruse your favorite silly website (nothing serious allowed!).
- Turn up the music and sing along, loudly!

When a Parent Has an Eating Disorder

Parenting a child with an eating disorder is painful. Parenting a child who has an eating disorder when you also have an eating disorder or are in recovery from an eating disorder is even more difficult. Many men and women have an eating disorder, and even more have some form of disordered eating. When a child has disordered eating, a parent's eating issues can be exacerbated and can bring up a host of physical, mental, and emotional concerns.

A Parent's Recovery

"I felt like I was in a bad afterschool movie. I was watching my daughter starve herself, search through her room for hidden diet pills, and kept her weekly therapy appointments for her eating disorder," said Anna. "I was the eating disorder police. I was doing everything right. I followed the steps I was supposed to take religiously. I was frustrated that it was taking so long to make a difference, and after weeks of hard work, I wasn't seeing any changes, or at least not significant ones.

"Meanwhile, while I was trying to take care of everything in the family, I let my own recovery go by the wayside. That's all it took for my own bulimia to come roaring back. The irony was not lost on me. I would worry about my daughter not eating and I would binge. I'd feel horrible about my binge, and then I'd go purge. It was this horrible craziness that I was humiliated about."

"Mothers especially need to recover for the sake of themselves, for their own value, for their own purpose, because we deserve it. Children may be the best motivators, the best inspiration, but guilt can't be the reason a parent recovers from an eating disorder," explains Dena Cabrera, PsyD, of Remuda Ranch. Coping with a child's eating disorder may well be triggering for a parent's unresolved eating disorder. It is naive to think that parents with an active eating disorder can effectively help their child if they are not dealing with their own issues. Getting help for oneself is a critical component of helping one's child.

Let Go of Guilt

So much of what parents hear on a regular basis revolves around guilt. "If you don't do this, your child will end up with this problem." "If they don't go to the right school, it's your fault." "If they aren't making their own beds by a certain age, they are going to grow up to be ax murderers." That guilt is especially difficult for mothers who have had an eating disorder and feel as though they may have "given" the eating disorder to their children.

"The moms I hear from are so terrified of passing on their own issues with food and body image that it is almost paralyzing," explains Katja Rowell, MD. "Self-doubt takes over. If they have a larger-than-average daughter, the fear of [her being] overweight or overreacting is almost overwhelming. They may not trust their instincts around feeding. They might be more likely to accept an expert's advice on pushing or restraining food even if on some level they know it isn't working. It makes it harder to trust the process, and to let the child control what she is supposed to control, that is, how much she is supposed to eat. Feeding a child can be incredibly triggering for a parent within the context of the current weight and nutrition hysteria. Fat mothers also describe feeling especially judged and vulnerable when feeding their children well. The fat mother who allows her child to have a child-sized portion of dessert at a restaurant may get looks or comments, even if the child is fed optimally and is healthy. There is way too much judgment around mothers and feeding in general."

Eating disorders are not contagious. Is it possible that a parent's unhealthy relationship with food and body image contributed to a child's eating disorder? Just the fact that a parent with an eating disorder passed along his genes boosts the child's odds of developing an eating disorder. When a parent is actively having disordered eating, it may well be contribute to a child's disordered eating. That being said, what's more important is what a parent does once a child has been diagnosed. Beating up oneself over and over again for "failing" helps no one, not the child or the parent.

"On the flip side," says Rowell, "I hear from mothers all the time who say that feeding their children well, in a trust model, has helped them in their recovery. When a child can stop halfway through a piece of cake because they are full, it's almost an epiphany for many moms. They think, 'If she can do that, maybe I can learn that, too.' I know for me on my journey to eating competence, that last step of really trusting my body happened while I was learning to feed my daughter well. If she could do it, so could I!"

A Parent's Food Issues

We all have issues with food, explains Ashley Solomon, PsyD. "Whether it's experiencing guilt about eating too much, feeling fear about keeping certain items in the home, or turning to a childhood staple when feeling stressed, food holds a multitude of meanings for each of us. There will likely be times in everyone's lives where their relationship with food gets distorted. Likewise, we live in a culture where beauty is currency and we are bombarded with thousands of implicit and explicit messages about our bodies each day. Even if a parent doesn't think she has a 'problem' per se, I believe it is worth exploring your own relationship with food and body image. Awareness and insight are incredibly valuable and can help foster a more honest relationship in the parent's self, as well as with her child."

An Honest Look

Many parents with an eating disorder do not think that their children are aware of what's going on. That isn't the case most of the time. Particularly with sensitive children, they may not know exactly what is happening, but they can pick up on deep anxiety and depression, especially as it is related to food and body perception.

Take a few minutes and reflect on these questions related to how your eating disorder has affected your family:

- How does my eating disorder take peace away from the dinner table?
- Where does my inflexibility affect my parenting?
- What am I trying to avoid?
- What do I need to do differently for myself?
- Do my children see me focusing on my body?
- Do my children see my lack of compassion for myself?
- Are my expectations of myself unreasonable?
- Are my expectations of my child unreasonable?

Make the Connection

Part of the reason a parent has an eating disorder is because it serves him or her in some way. It allows the person to escape some pain. As a parent, it is important to consider ways that hiding behind an eating disorder serves as an escape. It's even more tempting to escape when family life is painful. However, the danger (beyond the damage to oneself) in getting lost in the eating disorder at this time is that when you are disconnected from yourself, you are disconnected from your children. This is a time in your child's life when he or she can least afford for you to disconnect.

One of the most powerful things that parents can do in the treatment of an eating disorder is to participate in family therapy. Not only will the therapy help parents learn about how to interact in the healthiest ways around issues of food and weight with their child, but it can be a safe space to begin addressing parents' own issues around these topics.

CHAPTER 17

The Rest of the Family

When your child has an eating disorder, it often feels as though that label suddenly defines your entire family. Whether parents are divorced or living in the same house, relationships get battered. Siblings can feel lost in the chaos as parents try to battle the eating disorder. Eating disorders change families, who often feel as though they must walk on eggshells to avoid additional conflict. Eating disorders will affect not only the family unit but all of the members of the family.

The Rest of the Family

When a child has an eating disorder, it is very challenging not to let the eating disordered family member disrupt the entire family. Family dinners aren't safe, vacations are iffy if eating meals out is difficult, even celebrations like birthdays become fraught with potential battles. The goal when living with a child with an eating disorder is that the rest of the family should go on with their lives as normally as possible. The tendency in a family with a disordered eater is to take the path of least resistance and allow the disordered eater to set the tone and rules for food and meals, not out of apathy, but out of a desperate attempt to maintain a sense of calm.

No Secrets Allowed

The emotional toll and constant struggle of an eating disorder in the family can leave parents exhausted and unable or unwilling to focus on other important relationships. When your child has a disease, that's when you need support the most. Telling people around you—whether it is extended family, colleagues, or friends—about your child's eating disorder can be difficult, especially because of outdated perceptions of eating disorders. As such, the natural tendency is to try to contain the problem and to keep the eating disorder a secret. Secrets don't help anyone, and they force family members to limit the scope of support they receive. The enemy to recovery is secrecy.

Set Boundaries

"It was not unusual for our family to go to bed at night and for my daughter to binge and eat almost everything in the house. Literally, we would get up in the morning and she would have eaten flour and sugar and raw noodles. It got to be where I locked up food at night. It's embarrassing to have a bicycle chain on the refrigerator, but it protected her from herself until she got better," says Evelina, whose daughter's bulimia started at twelve.

The types of rules your family sets will depend on the nature of the eating disorder and how it manifests itself in your child. "I don't clean toilets that she's thrown up in, either," explains Evelina. "That's her responsibility. I work very hard to make sure she isn't alone for at least an hour after she eats, but if she does purge, I won't clean up after her. She needs to live with the very real consequences of her disorder, even if it's unpleasant."

Often, people with eating disorders will nurture others while denying their own very real need for food. Ironically, the person with disordered eating will often want to shop, cook for, and feed the family while either binging or starving themselves. One of the ways families can begin to take control of the eating disorder is to refuse to allow the eating disordered family member to dominate the rest of the family's eating patterns any longer. Families should go on with normal eating patterns. The disordered eater can no longer take any responsibility for shopping or cooking for the family. That's part of the disease, and it can't be tolerated.

When Partners Disagree

No two parental caregivers will agree all of the time on what to do and how to handle a child with an eating disorder. Just as conflict in any relationship is inevitable, so is conflict over the best treatment for a child with an eating disorder. "There are times I feel like a prisoner in my own home," explains Thom. "For years, our entire life revolved around what our daughter will or won't eat, what she does or doesn't weigh, what she can and can't cope with. My wife wants to cater to her every whim, and I am not willing to anymore. I've thought about leaving, but I don't know what to do anymore."

Consider the Source

Just like a savvy enemy, eating disorders have an insidious way of finding the cracks in a family, explains eating disorder therapist Ashley Solomon, PsyD. "If there are rifts in the family or between the parents, the eating disorder will use these to its advantage and become stronger. The danger is that if parents are beaten down from the often physical and emotional exhaustion that comes with supporting a child through this, the eating disorder can become stronger." When you feel yourself feeling overwhelmed and frustrated, that's when you need to reach out to others for support—either to your partner, to your friends and family, or to professionals. Don't let the pain of the eating disorder cause you to isolate yourself. It won't help you, your family, or your child.

When Sides Collide

There are times when parents may strongly disagree about medical decisions. When parents are married, living together, or separated, then medical treatment consent of either parent is usually sufficient. If a parent has never married or is divorced, then the parent who has sole legal custody generally has the power to make medical treatment decisions unless ordered otherwise by a judge. If two parents strongly disagree about the treatment path, then one of the parents may choose to petition a court to ask a judge to intervene and make a decision.

Particularly if you do not live with the other biological parent of your child, look for ways to make the eating disorder treatment process go as smoothly as possible. You should place a copy of any legal papers, including divorce decrees, custody papers, and visitation rights, in your child's medical record with all health care providers. If one of the parents cannot be present for a meeting, then share notes or a tape recording of information. Ask for two copies of all lab tests, clinical reports, and teaching materials so both parents have the same information.

Helping Siblings

Unfortunately, eating disorder shrapnel spares no one in the family. If there are other children in your family, it is quite likely they are experiencing difficulty with their sibling's eating disorder. When one child has an emotional or physical crisis, the other children in the family are likely to feel left out and alone. There is little available research on either the effects of eating disorders on siblings or how to best support those siblings.

What Do I Say?

You will have to make the decision about how much information to share with your child's siblings. Obviously, there are significant factors involved, including the age and developmental ability of your other children. Your children will be aware that something is happening. What you may not realize is that even if you do not specifically tell your other children what is happening, they may suspect the worst and may even blame themselves for the tension and frustration in the household. The siblings may feel empathy toward their hurting sibling and may want to help but have no idea how to do so.

 Essential

Ask family members or friends to help out by taking siblings on special outings, such as to the mall, sports activities, church, or just out for a walk sometimes. Every person in the family needs a safe space where true feelings can be expressed without fear of judgment or criticism.

For most people, including children, knowing what is happening in your family can be a relief, even though the specific facts can be difficult to understand. Even as a parent, eating disorders can feel incomprehensible. To a child, it can seem terrifying. When your other children know what is happening with their sibling, good things can happen. They can reduce their anxiety levels, feel like an important member of the family, and can even be included in family plans and discussions, as age and developmentally appropriate. When talking to your children, include information about the eating disorder, what is happening now, and how you are going to proceed with treatment for the eating disorder. The information that you provide should, of course, be appropriate for the maturity and age of the child. If you aren't sure what to say, you may want to consider talking to another parent or health care professional. Reassure them that you are doing everything you can to get treatment for their sibling.

How Siblings Feel

When a child has a life-threatening eating disorder, the feelings of a sibling can sometimes be ignored or minimized. Siblings of a child with an eating disorder often feel resentful and frustrated that their sibling has taken center stage in the family and there seems to be little attention left over for them. At the same time, siblings may also feel guilty for wanting attention, especially in light of the brother or sister's obvious needs. It's a difficult quandary—to feel needs, have those needs be unmet, and then to feel guilty for having those needs. Feelings of loss and loneliness are also common feelings because their previous relationship with the sibling has undoubtedly changed and will be limited by the eating disorder. They may also be worried that they will develop an eating disorder.

 Essential

As much as possible, once a week if you can, carve out even a brief amount of time for each sibling to spend time with a parent alone and engaged in a fun activity, whether it's walking the dog, playing a card game, or competing on Wii.

Support the Siblings

Because other children may feel alone, it is important to be aware of how much of your time, energy, and emotions are being directed toward your child with the eating disorder. As difficult as it may be, find ways to spend one-on-one time with your other children that have absolutely nothing to do with eating disorders. Go to a ball game, study spelling words, take a walk, snuggle at the end of the day, and focus exclusively on what is happening with your other child. Not only will your other children appreciate it, it will probably do you good as well.

 Fact

Make a concerted effort to reach out to all of your children with an affectionate touch, a warm hug, and a sincere "I love you," "I am proud of you," and "I care for you." Those intentional moments of love and emotional support are important for everyone in your family.

How to Respond

It is important to let siblings know that anything their sibling says or does should not be taken personally. They need to hear that their brother or sister has a disease and that his or her erratic behaviors are not a reflection of his or her feelings toward the rest of the family but are instead a reflection of the disease. If you live with a child with an eating disorder, even in recovery, extreme behavior is not uncommon, including tears, screams, temper tantrums, and assorted fit-throwing. Parents are more likely to be able to put the behavior in perspective and understand that the heightened responses are the disease speaking and come from feeling out of control and scared. Those strong emotions can be frightening to other children, and you can help them create a plan for what they should do during these difficult times. You might tell siblings that their help is not needed during the situation and that when it begins they should go to their room, read a book, listen to music, or watch television, for example.

Post a few phone numbers of special adult friends whom they can call if they are feeling scared or overwhelmed while you are busy coping with an outburst. They need to be able to find a safe space when they feel overwhelmed. Again, it is critical to reassure your other children that recovery from an eating disorder creates a significant amount of anxiety, but this is only temporary. Remind them that this will get better and you will do whatever it takes to help the sibling stay and feel safe.

Normalcy Matters

As you look toward setting short- and long-term goals for your family, keep in mind that siblings need to be able to continue to develop along their own path. For a child with disordered eating, it can actually be very helpful to see his or her healthy sibling's progress. A sibling who continues to go on living life, enjoying sports and other hobbies, time with friends, and has a normal relationship with food can be an excellent example. "I wanted what she had," said Marna, speaking of her sister, Maria. "Maria went to school and hung out with friends and laughed. It seemed simple, but it really helped me to look at her and see what I wanted to get back."

Help the other children maintain healthy relationships with other family members and with their peers. Maintain normal activities as much as possible. Other siblings in the family have the right to feel as though they belong, that home is safe, and that eating together as a family can be pleasurable. That won't happen all the time, but it is a worthy goal to continue to strive for in your family.

 Essential

If your children are having a difficult time making sense of the eating disorder, and you are concerned they are becoming more withdrawn, are acting out more, or seem to need extra support, consider getting individual counseling for them as well.

When the Dinner Table Is a Battlefield

One has not truly had a bad dinner until one has battled with a child with an eating disorder at the kitchen table. Even in the best of times, family dinners can be chaotic, messy, and unorganized. When a child has an eating disorder, it can be hellish. Especially when a child is in the refeeding phase, it can be exhausting. When a child with an eating disorder complains, whines, or even screams in frustration, it can be tempting to give in and do whatever it takes to make the drama stop, even if just for the night.

"The mantra I live with is that 'food is medicine.' Food is medicine. If I ever get a tattoo, that's what it will say. I reminded myself and my partner and my daughter over and over again whenever one of us was ready to give up. If my daughter had cancer and needed chemotherapy and begged me not to make her take it, I would have to tell her that I am sorry, but that she needs the chemotherapy to get better. That we'd have to live with being uncomfortable and even in some pain, but we would do what we needed to do to save her life. The same is true with her eating disorder. Food is medicine and when she's malnourished, she can't think as well. She no longer has the ability to choose what she eats and how much she eats. This won't be forever, but this is what we're living with right now," explains Diane.

Family Meal Tips

There are steps you can take to increase the enjoyment of family meals. Weather permitting, eat outside. If weather doesn't permit, have a picnic in the living room. Light candles, don't harp about table manners, and ban electronic devices, including TV, phones, and any other handheld devices. No texting allowed!

Other tips to try during meals:

- Listen to music
- Tell jokes
- Share the best thing that happened during the day
- Talk about interests or enjoyable activities
- Ask one thing that was learned today, and even have the adults participate
- Look for ways to laugh together; if food is medicine, then laughter is a bandage

CHAPTER 18

Chasing Recovery

Recovering from an eating disorder is not like recovering from most other diseases. If you have a virus, you get the right medication and then you get cured. Even with cancer, there comes a point after treatment where you get blood work drawn or an MRI and you are declared cancer-free. There is no such moment in eating disorders. How do you know how to help your child who is in recovery?

What Recovery Means

What recovery means for your child depends on your understanding of your child's needs. Chasing a number on a scale is rarely enough to declare victory—as anyone knows who has ever tried to lose weight. Do nothing to change the underlying cause for the weight gain, and within a few weeks and months, the weight is back on. The same is true with an eating disorder. While physical changes are important, the emotional changes must also occur for true recovery.

"My recovery started when I decided to tell my boyfriend at age twenty-two. I was scared and thought he would look down on me. I felt ashamed and guilty. Telling him was one of the best decisions in my life. I now know that an eating disorder is a real, life-threatening illness. It is nothing to be ashamed of or to feel guilty about. I got professional help (a treatment team of a psychiatrist, internist, therapist, dietitian, and various support groups) and began the road to recovery. My family and friends were critical in my healing as well. My parents participated in family therapy, and together we learned ways that they could best support me. Mostly, my family just had to support me, love me, and believe me. When I said, 'I feel fat,' they believed that was my experience. They didn't understand it, but that didn't matter. They never needed to understand my eating disorder. They just needed to believe my experience. And they did," explains Jenni Schaefer, author of *Goodbye Ed, Hello Me.*

Eye on the Prize

"One of the things I wish someone had told me was not to bother spinning my wheels on questions related to why. At first, I believed what everyone around me was saying about having to know why she had the eating disorder before we could treat it. It wasn't true. The cancer analogy keeps coming back to me; if she had a tumor, it would be removed immediately so it won't metastasize and take over more of her body. The surgeon does not have to know why the tumor was there to operate and remove it. Just like with cancer, the sooner you intervene, the better your child's chances for recovery. Once we got her on the road to recovery, then we could deal with underlying issues," explained Hannah, whose daughter has been recovered for several years.

 Essential

> Even when it comes to recovery, parents too often look to medical professionals to tell them what to do and when their child is "fixed." Whenever you want a doctor to tell you what to do, you've lost faith in yourself and overestimated the power of a medical degree.

It is critical to resist the temptation to try to understand the reasons behind the problem initially; meanwhile, the child in crisis is continuing to binge, purge, starve, or overexercise, and his or her mental and physical health deteriorates. The causes are an important part of eating disorder treatment, but they are simply a part of the treatment, not the initial focus or even the primary goal.

Identifying Recovery

"My advice to teens and their parents is, first and foremost, to believe that it is possible to be fully recovered (period)," Jenni Schaefer explains. Believing that recovery is possible is one thing. Understanding what that looks like is another. To make matters more confusing, recovery may look totally different to a nutritionist, a physician, and a psychologist. What is recovery from an eating disorder? Is it simply weight restoration? Or is it when the person no longer meets the diagnostic criteria for an eating disorder? Is it simply stopping the unwanted behavior? The core goals of recovery are based on individual needs and, ideally, should be agreed upon by the parents and primary members of the health care team. Recovery goals may include:

- Achieve a healthy and sustainable body weight
- Develop healthy, nondieting eating habits
- Learn to integrate healthy activity into one's life
- Treat physical complications that have occurred due to unhealthy eating or weight control practices
- Treat psychological problems such as anxiety or depression
- Provide tools to replace unhealthy thoughts with healthier ones and to challenge irrational thinking that maintains eating disorders
- Gradually introduce more autonomy regarding lifestyle and nutrition

Recovery Is More Than a Number

Understanding what eating disorder recovery isn't is just as important, and maybe even more so, than looking at what eating disorder recovery is. From a traditional medical system approach, treatment of an eating disordered individual is based on weight restoration, or at least medical stabilization. True recovery is not based on a single ideal number, or even lab tests that measure nutritional status. Recovery is not limited to:

- Getting a BMI over 17.5
- An acceptable minimum weight
- Weight level reached when period or nocturnal emissions return
- A specific date when healing occurs

Eating disorder recovery is a highly individual process, and it is an indicator of rejoining one's normal functioning. It also marks the continuation of very hard work. Even if your child is released from medical care, take the long view on treating your child's eating disorder.

Letting Go of Misconceptions

Common misconceptions of treating an eating disorder are that the underlying causes of an eating disorder have to be treated in order to pursue recovery, or that weight restoration equals recovery. These aren't the only misconceptions that can hinder a child's recovery from an eating disorder. One of the most dangerous ones is that a child needs to "choose" to recover and that she won't recovery until she is ready. While at some point compliance is necessary, it isn't necessary for the parents to begin or continue treatment. If parents believe that their child will stop restricting, purging, or bingeing when she is ready to do so, they may wait to act until that point, and irreversible physical harm may occur. Lastly, a common thinking error is that eating disorders can be treated without full nutrition, and it simply cannot. Logical and healthy thinking requires a brain and body that is well-nourished.

The Bumpy Road to Recovery

You've accepted the fact your daughter has an eating disorder. You have been to the physician and gotten blood work, a thorough physical, and a diagnosis, and you have a treatment plan with a nutritionist and counselor. Recovery should start any day now, right? What the pros may forget to tell you is that not only is your child likely to be noncompliant, but when you stop behavior that an eating disordered person has come to depend on, expect resistance as she experiences real symptoms of physical and emotional withdrawal. Withdrawal is unavoidable, but fortunately it is not permanent.

 Essential

The first thing you must do, without exception, is to get rid of your scale. Recovery cannot happen if your child has access to a scale. At least initially, weight will fluctuate quickly and may panic patients early in recovery. This goes for measuring tapes, too.

Physical Withdrawal Symptoms

Whether your child binges and purges, compulsively overeats, or starves herself, there will be physical symptoms when she returns to normal eating. For a compulsive overeater, expect your child to experience extreme hunger, difficulty sleeping, even fatigue and nausea. Keep your child busy and well-hydrated to help minimize side effects. For those who have a history of purging and can no longer do so, they may experience feeling bloated, constipation, weight gain of a few pounds, electrolyte imbalances, and nausea. Those who have limited their food intake and are now eating more may experience constipation, a lack of hunger signals, and difficulty sleeping. They will think they are not hungry because they have not listened to their own body's signals for a period of time.

Most people who begin eating disorder treatment can expect some physical withdrawal symptoms, either related to giving up old habits or beginning new ones. Think of it like an alcoholic undergoing withdrawal. It may be difficult physically, but it is valuable to go through the process for the long-term benefits.

Emotional Withdrawal

You can also expect your child with disordered eating to go through an emotional or mental withdrawal process. At times, your child may feel overpowering emotions of depression, anxiety, anger, sadness, and feeling overwhelmed. After all, the eating disorder served, in some ways, as a means of numbing or hiding from any negative feelings. When you take away the ability to hide from those feelings, facing them for the first time in a while can feel overwhelming and difficult. Difficult for your child and for everyone around her. People who detox from alcohol or drugs go through the same painful process of learning to once again live with their feelings, thoughts, and emotions that were once so painful.

"My first instinct was to ease my son into treatment and help him adjust slowly. I would start limiting the number of times he could purge or say he could skip some meals but not others. It was this crazy approach that had me negotiating the most ridiculous things. There's a reason they say you can't negotiate with a terrorist. I had to finally decide that the eating disorder would find no safe harbor in our family. There was no skipping meals, there was no purging, there was no letting Brad stay a little bit ensnared. Ripping off the bandage all at once was much more effective," says Brad's mom, Eliza. "Yes, he was mad. Yes, he was upset. Yes, he was crabby, irritable, threw fits, and acted ridiculous. But he also stopped. We lived through it and the emotions became more manageable, and Brad came to count on our firm expectations and steadfastness."

Recovery Peers

Do what it takes to help your child build a recovery peer group. For some, an online recovery peer group will provide enough support. For others, a real-time group may be better at holding your child accountable. Many people who struggle with compulsive overeating and bulimia turn to Overeaters Anonymous, and it is free. Many eating disorder associations list current support groups, and your mental health care professional should be aware of what is available in your area.

 Essential

Keep in mind that if you are in a relationship where the other person (parent, child, sibling, friend, partner, etc.) is addicted, Alanon and Naranon can be excellent resources even if the person's addiction is not limited to substances.

Stick with Winners

Make sure you surround yourself with plenty of people who are on the road to recovery. There's a twelve-step phrase that says, "Stick with the winners." Make sure the people you are with are actually winners; in other words, stick with other people who are committed to making a full recovery. There is a tendency to want to stay close with people who are struggling because it can make you feel better about your own progress or because you think you can help them. Remind your child as many times as necessary that there are other people who are better equipped to help those who are still struggling with an eating disorder. Being close to someone who is not doing well in recovery will not serve your child well. When you surround yourself with people who think in ways that are dangerous and unhealthy, you begin to think those thoughts are normal and recovery ground can be lost.

Fact

Mentor Connect is a free resource that provides mentors to people with eating disorders to help them to break through the isolation of eating disorders by sharing the tools of recovery in supporting relationships. To learn more, go to *www.mentorconnect-ed.org.*

Emergency Plan

Help your child create an emergency phone list, and keep it with him at all times. On the top of this list should be the therapist and other health care providers, as needed. If your child is involved in a twelve-step program, his sponsor should be on there, too. Fill in the rest of the list with people who are supportive of your child's recovery until your child has a list of at least ten names and contact numbers whom your child can call when he or she fears recovery is at stake.

Numbers that may be helpful include:

- Hope Line Network 800-273-TALK
- National Suicide Hotline 800-SUICIDE (800-784-2433)
- Massachusetts Eating Disorder Association, Inc. Helpline 1-617-558-1881
- Bulimia and Self-Help Hotline 1-314-588-1683
- Self-Injury Help by S.A.F.E. (Self-Abuse Finally Ends) 1-800-DONT CUT (1-800-366-8288)

Prepared = Protected

While your child needs to work through issues about perfectionism, body image, and control with a counselor, there are plenty of ways you can stay involved and help your child as he or she continues the recovery process. Continue to meet regularly with your child's counselor and stay connected to the counseling process so you are aware of what is happening and can continue to make changes in family dynamics and processes as needed. As your child hits bumps in the road, there are ways you can step in to encourage and restore your child's faith in his or her abilities, resources, and gifts.

 Fact

> There are a number of books, workbooks, and other resources on the market that may be helpful or that your child can work through with you or a therapist. *The Slender Trap* by Lauren Stern is an excellent workbook to help teenagers look at the way they see their bodies and their expectations of themselves.

Affirmation

The very idea of affirmations may sound cheesy. But anyone who has struggled with an eating disorder has also struggled with feeling inadequate, less than, and somehow just not enough—not pretty enough, not smart enough, not loved enough, or not strong enough. When someone is in recovery from an eating disorder and those old coping mechanisms are taken away, those feelings can be particularly strong, and your child may not know how to combat those feelings of inadequacy.

Help your child make a list of at least ten different affirmations that have nothing to do with how he looks. Don't make the list for your child or he won't believe it. Create it together, and don't worry; you don't need to come up with some elaborate and over-the-top affirmations. They should be as basic as necessary to create good feelings about your child. Your child doesn't have to believe them at this moment, she just has to believe that they are potentially true. State all affirmations in a positive way. In other words, avoid using negative statements like "I will not purge." Here are some affirmation examples to get you started:

- I have the right to be accepted for who I am.
- I am worthy of love.
- I care about myself.
- I am capable.
- I can handle it when things go wrong.
- I deserve good physical and emotional health.
- I am responsible for my own happiness.
- I have the support I need.
- I accept support when I need it. I accept peace and joy in all aspects of my life.
- My intention is to live free from struggle, fear, and hopelessness.
- I make every act an act of love (or freedom or hope, etc.). I am powerful. I am worthy. I am free.
- I am whole and perfect, and my seeming imperfections are what make me beautiful.
- My life has purpose and meaning.
- I nourish myself every day.
- I give and receive love unconditionally.
- I can be honest with my feelings.
- I can let go of being compulsive.
- I can let go of fear.
- I am courageous.
- I can grow.
- I can handle all changes that come my way.

All of these affirmations can be changed to fit the needs of your child. Your child may want to pick a few favorites to focus on, then work down the list. Or he may want to write his affirmation on a 3 x 5 index card and place it where it can be seen as a daily reminder of a positive aspect about himself. Every time your child sees these affirmation cards, they will remind your child to agree with that statement and think and act in ways that make that statement a reality.

Develop a Mantra

"You need to create a mantra that works for you. I always said 'I am worth it' when I was struggling with giving in. My sponsor used the phrase 'I love me.' Other people I know who were in recovery from addiction used phrases like 'I can do this,' 'I'll do it for me,' and 'Easy does it,'" explained Emily, who attended twelve-step meetings as a part of her recovery.

Not everyone wants a top ten list of affirmations; some need useful phrases—mantras—that they can count on to remind them what to focus on when recovery is difficult. Alcoholics Anonymous has a number of sayings that people recovering from disordered eating may find useful when struggling.

- It gets better.
- Pain is the touchstone of progress.
- The mind is like a parachute: it works better when it's open.
- We have a disease that tells us we don't have a disease.
- Just for today.
- One day at a time.
- First things first.
- I got sick of being sick and tired.
- It's easy to talk the talk, but you have to walk the walk.
- Gratitude is an attitude.

 Essential

Encourage your child to make a God box (or the name of any other higher power as preferred). This may sound silly, but every time something feels difficult or overwhelming, write it on a slip of paper and drop it in your God box to practice accepting difficulties instead of focusing on them.

Understanding Triggers

One of the most important things a person with disordered eating can do is to know what triggers his or her disordered eating. This is also true for the parent of someone with disordered eating. With time, when you know your child's symptoms, you can probably recognize a slip coming. It may seem obvious to a parent or outsider, but often young people do not recognize their own disordered thinking, anxiety, frustration, or maladaptive behaviors. Remember, this isn't an eating problem, it's an emotional and cognitive problem. When you see those symptoms erupt, you can help your child become aware of them so you can help interrupt the process.

Here's an example of how to interrupt the process. Claire, a compulsive overeater, had just gotten in a fight with her older brother Kyle that ended with Kyle slamming the door in her face and telling her never to come in his room again. A few minutes later, Claire's mom found her in the kitchen, rummaging through the pantry for food.

"What's going on, Claire?" asked her mother.

"Nothing, I'm just hungry," said Claire, still looking for food.

"I heard Kyle yelling at you. Sounds like he was pretty angry."

"I hate him," said Claire. "All I did was borrow his iPod and he acts like it's the end of the world."

"He does seem mad you took it without permission, which isn't cool, but you just had lunch, so I'm wondering why you think you're hungry."

"I don't know." Claire shrugged. "I just am."

"I think you might be upset and it might feel like hunger. Let's go play a game, and when we're done, if you're still hungry, we'll make some popcorn."

Unhealthy Thoughts

People with eating disorders tend to think in very black and white—there is no middle ground. They feel either fat or thin, good or bad, happy or suicidal. Part of helping a child go through recovery is making him aware of when he is acting on those feelings. For a child who is a perfectionist, for example, a grade or sports event can create very strong feelings of self-loathing. Being in recovery doesn't mean those thoughts won't arise, but when they do, it involves being able to say, "Well, I am disappointed that I didn't score higher, but it's not a big deal. I really enjoy that class or that sport, and not being perfect in it is okay." Learning to direct those thoughts in smaller areas can help when more serious thoughts erupt, like these:

- "I'm running late and I don't have time for breakfast, I can skip it today."
- "I'm in training and lots of people exercise for hours at a time."
- "I've got this under control enough that I can go back on a reasonable diet."
- "I feel constipated and I need to get some laxatives."
- "I feel really good and I don't need to keep taking my medication."

For people with an eating disorder, those thoughts, or ones that are similar, will arise, and your child needs to be prepared to recognize those thoughts as unhealthy and damaging. If a child with an eating disorder can capture those thoughts, look at them, and reject them as no longer valid, then that is an important step toward recovery.

 Essential

Encourage your child to keep a journal, especially once he or she is on the way to recovery. Once your child starts putting thoughts down on paper, patterns can emerge and your child can be more aware of emotions, thoughts, and fears and work through them with a counselor, parent, or other support person.

Unhealthy Behaviors

If your child doesn't catch his unhealthy thoughts when they first emerge, then the unhealthy behaviors may start soon afterward. The way your child thinks about a situation often initiates a response. For example, if your child isn't feeling good about himself right now, he may start buying magazines that are problematic, such as *Shape*, *Muscle*, *Vogue*, or other fashion- or exercise-focused topics. Other behaviors that are warning signs include sleeping too much, withdrawing from friends or family, or exercising more than usual. Such behaviors indicate that a checkup is in order and closer vigilance is necessary, at least for the short term.

 Fact

Encourage your child to make a list of internal and external triggers, including scales, bathing suits, certain television shows, unwanted sexual attention, etc. Teach your child to be aware of what happens internally when those triggers occur.

Imperfect Recovery

There isn't a perfect blueprint for the ideal recovery from an eating disorder. Recovery is guaranteed to have its ups and down along the way. You will probably go through several different members on your treatment team before you meet the ones who are best able to serve your family. You will probably get frustrated and feel overwhelmed during times when progress, which can take weeks, months, and sometimes years (though those cases are few and far between), seems nonexistent or agonizingly slow. You will doubt your ability to make the best decisions and your child's ability to recover fully. Those are all normal parts of the recovery process.

Imperfect Parents

You will likely stumble on your child's path to recovery. You will probably make mistakes, even big ones. You might yell at your child, beg, or threaten, but the world won't end and your own journey to becoming an effective parent of an ill child continues. Imperfect parents can still help their children through recovery.

You do the best you can with the resources you have. When you feel overwhelmed, get more help. If you feel like you aren't on the right path, explore different options. Just don't give up on your child; keep believing that recovery is possible at any point.

Imperfectly Perfect

Recovery simply means that your child can live life again and have a healthy relationship with her body and herself. Your daughter may never be the ideal weight that some chart says she should weigh. She may always be twenty pounds more or less than somebody else's ideals. He may never feel that his body is a perfect specimen of male physique. But if your son or daughter can experience strong emotions of great sadness or anxiety and still find a way to walk through it without binging or starving, and get to peace, then that's what recovery looks like.

Genifer looks back on her journey with an eating disorder: "I am now thirty-six years old. I have ruined my kidneys and my bowels don't work properly. I also have two beautiful children. I tell my children every day how beautiful they are, how smart they are, and how capable they are. I encourage their interests, wholeheartedly. I enjoy my food. I love eating. I can now look at my husband in the face and say, 'I'm hungry. I want to eat something.'"

Recommended Reading

Introductory Reading

The Dieter's Dilemma: Eating Less and Weighing More, William Bennett

Jane Brody's Nutrition Book, Jane E. Brody

The Eating Disorder Sourcebook: A Comprehensive Guide to the Causes, Treatments, and Prevention of Eating Disorders, Carolyn Costin

Making Peace with Food, Susan Kano

Breaking the Diet Habit: The Natural Weight Alternative, Janet Polivy

Specific Eating Disorders

Overcoming Night Eating Syndrome: A Step-by-Step Guide to Breaking the Cycle, Kelly C. Allison, Albert J. Stunkard, and Sara L. Thier

Overcoming Binge Eating, Christopher G. Fairburn

Bulimia: A Guide to Recovery, Lindsey Hall and Leigh Cohn

Boys Get Anorexia Too: Coping with Male Eating Disorders in the Family, Jenny Langley

EDNOS: Eating Disorders Not Otherwise Specified: Scientific and Clinical Perspectives on the Other Eating Disorders, Claes Norring and Bob Palmer

The Adonis Complex: How to Identify, Treat, and Prevent Body Obsession in Men and Boys, Harrison G. Pope

The Binge Eating & Compulsive Overeating Workbook: An Integrated Approach to Overcoming Disordered Eating (Whole-Body Healing), Carolyn Coker Ross

Dying to Be Thin: Understanding and Defeating Anorexia and Bulimia, Ira Sacker and Marc Zimmer

Anorexia Nervosa: A Survival Guide for Families, Friends, and Sufferers, Janet Treasure

Treatment Resources

My Kid Is Back, June Alexander

Eating with Your Anorexic: How My Child Recovered Through Family-Based Treatment and Yours Can Too, Laura Collins

The Starving Family: Caregiving Mothers and Fathers Share Their

Eating Disorder Wisdom, Cheryl Dellasega, PhD

Treatment Manual for Anorexia Nervosa: A Family-Based Approach, James Lock MD PhD, Daniel Le Grange PhD, W. Stewart Agras MD, Christopher Dare, et al.

The Clinician's Guide to Collaborative Caring in Eating Disorders: The New Maudsley Method, Janet Treasure, Ulrike Schmidt, and Pam Macdonald

Skills-Based Learning for Caring for a Loved One with an Eating Disorder: The New Maudsley Method, Janet Treasure, Gráinne Smith, and Anna Crane

Off the C.U.F.F. (Calm, Unwavering, Firm, and Funny): A Parent Skills Book for the Management of Disordered Eating, Nancy Zucker, PhD

Resources for Children, Teens, and Parents

Afraid to Eat: Children and Teens in Weight Crisis, Frances M. Berg

Food Fight: A Guide to Eating Disorders for Preteens and Their Parents, Janet Bode

The Big Happy Bear: For Children of All Sizes, Betsy Bogert

What to Do When You're Sad & Lonely: A Guide for Kids, James J. Crist

Am I Fat? Helping Young Children Accept Differences in Body Size, Joanne P. Ikeda and Priscilla Naworski

Appetite for Life: Inspiring Stories of Recovery from Anorexia, Bulimia, and Compulsive Overeating, Margie Ryerson

Surviving an Eating Disorder: Strategies for Family and Friends, Michele Siegel, Judith Brisman, and Margor Weinshel

Body Image and Self-Esteem

Real Gorgeous: The Truth About Body and Beauty, Kaz Cooke

Real Girl Real World: A Guide to Finding Your True Self, Heather M. Gray and Samantha Phillips

Cleavage: Breakaway Fiction for Real Girls, Deb Loughead and Jocelyn Shipley

This Is Who I Am: Our Beauty in All Shapes and Sizes, Rosanne Olson

Celebrating Girls: Nurturing and Empowering Our Daughters, Virginia Beane Rutter

For Schools and Coaches

How Did This Happen? A Practical Guide to Understanding Eating Disorders—for Coaches, Parents, and Teachers, The Institute for Research & Education

How Schools Can Help Combat Student Eating Disorders, Michael P. Levine

Little Girls in Pretty Boxes: The Making and Breaking of Elite Gymnasts and Figure Skaters, Joan Ryan

APPENDIX B

Organizational Resource List

Academy for Eating Disorders
111 Deer Lake Road, Suite 100
Deerfield, IL 60015
847-498-4274
www.aedweb.org
Professional organization that
provides useful resources.

**American Academy of Child
and Adolescent Psychiatry**
3615 Wisconsin Avenue, N.W.
Washington, DC 20016-3007
202-966-7300
www.aacap.org
Information for psychiatrists
and families about developmental, behavioral, emotional,
and mental disorders affecting
children and adolescents.

American Dietetic Association
120 South Riverside Plaza
Suite 2000
Chicago, IL 60606-6995
800-877-1600
www.eatright.org
Nutrition information, resources,
and referral information
for registered dietitians.

**Association for Behaviorial
and Cognitive Therapies**
305 7th Avenue, 16th Fl.
New York, NY 10001
212-647-1890
www.aabt.org
Provides information and referrals
for cognitive behavioral therapists.

**Binge Eating Disorder
Association, Inc.**
637 Emerson Place
Severna Park, MD 21146
443-597-0066
www.bedaonline.com
Information and resources on
treatment for binge eating disorder.

The Body Positive
2550 Ninth St., Suite 204B
Berkeley, CA 94710
510-528-0101
www.thebodypositive.org
Uses educational materials to
help people adopt the Health
at Every Size philosophy, which
allows them to enjoy healthy
eating and physical activity in their natural body.

**Families Empowered and
Supporting Treatment
of Eating Disorders**
P.O. Box 331
Warrenton, VA 20188
540-227-8518
www.feast-ed.org

Fed-Up Girl
Los Angeles, CA
310-883-4135
www.fedupgirl.org
Nonprofit foundation that edu-
cates young girls on body image,
self-esteem, and balanced living
to prevent eating disorders.

FINDINGbalance, Inc.
P.O. Box 284
Franklin, TN 37065
615-599-6948
www.findingbalance.com
A faith-based nonprofit organization dedicated to helping
those who struggle with eating
and body image issues, particularly EDNOS (eating disorder not otherwise specified).

**Food Addicts in Recovery
Anonymous**
400 W. Cummings Park, Suite 1700
Woburn, MA 01801
781-932-6300
www.foodaddicts.org
A program of recovery is based
on the Twelve Steps and Twelve
Traditions of Alcoholics Anonymous. An international fellowship
of men and women who make
use of AA principles to gain
freedom from addictive eating.

Gürze Books
www.bulimia.com
A publishing company spe-
cializing in resources for eating disorders recovery.

Jessie's Wish
742 Colony Forest Drive
Midlothian, VA 23114
804-378-3032
www.jessieswish.org
A nonprofit organization committed to helping educate about eating disorders and raise funds to help with financial assistance when there is inadequate or no health insurance available.

National Association of Anorexia Nervosa and Associated Disorders
P.O. Box 640
Naperville, IL 60566
630-577-1330
www.anad.org
Nonprofit organization that provides details of support programs, treatment centers, and insurance-related issues.

National Eating Disorders Association
603 Stewart Street, Suite 803
Seattle, WA 98101
1-800-931-2237
www.nationaleatingdisorders.org
The NEDA organizes programs, conferences, and educational events related to eating disorders as well as an advocacy program.

National Institute of Mental Health
6001 Executive Boulevard
Bethesda, MD 20892
www.nimh.nih.gov
Largest scientific organization in the world focusing on mental health issues, and the website provides an excellent overview on many eating-disorder-related topics.

Web Resources

Eating Disorder Hope

www.eatingdisorderhope.com
The site provides eating disorder treatment options, support groups, articles, recovery tools, and more for individuals struggling with bulimia, anorexia, and binge eating disorder.

ED Referral

www.edreferral.com
Comprehensive database of anorexia, bulimia, and other eating disorder professionals.

Maudsley Parents

www.maudsleyparents.org
A volunteer organization dedicated to help families help their children through family-based treatment.

Men Get Eating Disorders Too

www.mengetedstoo.co.uk
A UK-based charity that aims to raise awareness of male eating disorders.

Mirror-Mirror

www.mirror-mirror.org
Resource site with specific info on athletes, men, and children with eating disorders; relapse warning signs; and much more.

Something Fishy

www.something-fishy.org
Thorough site with information and resources pertaining to anorexia, bulimia, and compulsive overeating.

Eating Disorder
Questionnaire

This is a screening measure to help you determine whether or not your child might have an eating disorder. This screening measure is not designed to diagnose an eating disorder or take the place of a professional diagnosis or consultation. For each item, indicate the extent to which it is true, not true, or if you are unsure, by checking the appropriate box next to the item.

	YES	NO	UNSURE
1. Does your child eat in secret, or hide or steal food?	☐	☐	☐
2. Does your child engage in self-injurious behavior, such as cutting, burning, or other methods?	☐	☐	☐
3. Does your child restrict food intake or eat very little, eat nothing, or try to eat as little as possible?	☐	☐	☐
4. Does your child binge, or eat large quantities of food in a short period of time?	☐	☐	☐
5. Does your child purge, or use methods such as self-induced vomiting or laxatives to attempt to get rid of what has been eaten?	☐	☐	☐
6. Does your child compulsively overeat even if not hungry?	☐	☐	☐

	YES	NO	UNSURE
7. Does your child compulsively exercise in a way that intrudes in life?	☐	☐	☐
8. Does your child take diet pills, laxatives, diuretics, or other pills or harmful substances to help curb appetite or get rid of calories?	☐	☐	☐
9. Does your child chew and spit by putting food in mouth, chewing it, and then spitting it out?	☐	☐	☐
10. Does your child suffer from a disruption in her menstrual cycle, sore throats, dental problems, common abdominal pain, insomnia, fatigue, and/or anxiety or depression?	☐	☐	☐
11. Does your child have certain rituals around eating that other people do not have?	☐	☐	☐
12. Has your child lost or gained weight (+,- ten pounds) in the last two months?	☐	☐	☐
13. Do your child's moods seem out of control and frequently change?	☐	☐	☐
14. Is it difficult for your child to eat in public?	☐	☐	☐

Score

Score 2 points for every Yes answer, and 1 point for every Unsure.

If your score is 6 or higher, it would be advisable and likely beneficial to seek a professional diagnosis from a trained health professional in your community.

If your score is less than 5, then your child may not have an eating disorder, but you should continue to monitor your child's behavior for other signs and symptoms of disordered eating.

Index